Making Dating & Quiz Games

Stephen Gose

Making Dating & Quiz Games

Stephen Gose

This book is for sale at http://leanpub.com/courses/leanpub/mbg-dating

This version was published on 2018-07-07

This is a Leanpub book. Leanpub empowers authors and publishers with the Lean Publishing process. Lean Publishing is the act of publishing an in-progress ebook using lightweight tools and many iterations to get reader feedback, pivot until you have the right book and build traction once you do.

© 2018 Stephen Gose

Contents

I Making Dating & Quiz Games 1
- Reference From: 1
- Overview 2
- Course Objectives: The Goal 2

1: Lesson: Game Mechanics 4
- Game Features 7
- Homework & Research: 7
- Dating Resources 7
- Exercise Lesson 1: 8
- Lesson 1 Quiz: 8

2: Lesson: Game Examples & Research 9
- Your competition in the Market 9
- Game Tools & Generators 9
- Homework & Research: 10
- Exercise 2: Develop a Unique Game 10
- Lesson 2 Quiz: 11

3: Lesson: Game Flow 12
- Network Impact 13
- Exercise 3: Network Research 16
- Lesson 3 Quiz: 17

CONTENTS

II Starting a Dating | Quiz Game Project 18

Project Files and Directories 18

Step 0: Review these demonstrations: 21

Step 1. Create our standard index file. 21

Step 2. Create your standard game scenes. 25

Step 3: Dating | Quiz Games' Logic & Supporting Functions 35

III Game #1 – Menza Mental Math™: a math tutor game. 38

Design Note: 38

Game #1 code review 39

Exercise Game 1: 39

4. Game #1 Supporting Functions 44

Exercise Game 1 Supporting Functions: 44

IV Game #2 – Tomfoolery Trivia Topics™ – a simple trivia game 47

Design Note: 48

Database Construction Tools 49

Creating various Languages 53

Game #2 code review 54

5. Game #2 Supporting Functions 57

Exercise Game 2 Supporting Functions: 58

answeredQ function – Lines 242 to 259 58

btnOver function – Lines 260 to 287 58

checkAnswer function – Lines 288 to 311 58

gameOver function – Lines 312 to 318 59

CONTENTS

  nextQuestion function – Lines 319 to 352 59

V Game #3 – Dating Veronica Darlene™ 60

  Design Notes: 61

  New conversation dialog format 62

  Conversation Dialog Sequence 63

  Creating various Languages 64

  Game 3 updated question format 65

  Game 3 JSON format Skeleton 66

  Game Pool Technology 69

  Art Resources 70

  Facial Expressions 71

  Game #3 code review 74

  Exercise Game 3: 75

6. **Game #3 Supporting Functions** 79

  Exercise Game 3 Supporting Functions: 79

  checkAnswer function – Lines 516 to 544 80

  clickContinue function – Lines 546 to 671 80

  gameOver function – Lines 674 to 678 80

  nextQuestion function – Lines 681 to 713 81

  Plugins 81

7. **Conclusion** 82

  More Game Starter Kit Tutorials 82

  Further Information 82

  Introduction References 83

VI Answers to Exercises 84

  Making Dating \& Quiz Games 84

CONTENTS

Game \#1 = Menza Mental Math™: a math tutor game. 84

Game \#2 = Tomfoolery Trivia Topics™ – a simple trivia game 85

Game \#3 = Dating Veronica Darlene™ 85

I Making Dating & Quiz Games

A *Starter Kit* Tutorial for Dating Simulations and Quiz Game Mechanics using *Phaser v2*

- Use the *Menu to navigate* between topic in the course.
- If you would like a *Course Completion Certificate*, please answer all the quiz questions at the end of each lesson.
- You will have *two chances to pass each end-of-lesson quiz*.
- You have a *limited number of attempts to complete this course*.
- There is *no expiration date* for this course.

Reference From:

This tutorial is a single chapter from a larger collection of 16 game mechanics found on http://leanpub.com/pgskc/

- Supporting website and bonus content: http://makingbrowsergames.com/starterkits/quiz/
- Game Design Workbook - https://leanpub.com/phaserjsgamedesignworkbook;
- Phaser Game Prototypes - https://leanpub.com/LoRD;
- Phaser Game Development Library - https://leanpub.com/b/phasergamedevelopment;
- Ultimate Phaser Library - https://leanpub.com/b/ultimatephaserlibrary

This tutorial is an abridged edition; it links to 276 additional pages of content. We chose this format to reduce the retail price while still supplying value. *In all, this tutorial is 317+ pages of total content*.

Overview

Dating & Quiz games are popular online games! Have you ever created an avatar? This Dating & Quiz Game tutorial is an easy-to-use blueprint for **Phaser.js JavaScript Gaming Framework** for either the official or Community Editions v2.x.x API; it has all the game mechanism and logic that you need for a complete *Dating & Quiz* game. Phaser is one of the best HTML5 / JavaScript game development frameworks on the Internet. It is certainly a powerful tool when combined with GUI-editors and Cocoon. Phaser liberates your design decisions since it is pure JavaScript. It gives complete freedom over your game design patterns, artwork selections, and your chosen deployment venues. I have been using Phaser Game Framework for quite some time now; and, have created this series of "Game Starter Kit & Blue Prints" which you might find beneficial in launching your own game projects. Furthermore, I created other game development tools to help me generate new game ideas.

Visit http://makingbrowsergames.com/gameDesigner/ and try them yourself.

You might wonder "why would anyone want to create such an online game?" Well, during my research for this chapter, I thought the same thing; **but, what I found is truly amazing.** Not only is "Dating & Quiz and Fashions" an ancient game mechanics, it also **boasts several patents and thousands of variations.**

Course Objectives: The Goal

I would like to guide you in creating *several styles of Dating & Quiz* games mechanics. We will use the game mechanics, mechanisms and the development methods discussed in *Phaser Game Prototypes.*[1] By the end of this tutorial, you should have three (3) fully functional *Dating & Quiz* games using your own generated assets. Here is the website where you can download the bonus content included with your course purchase.

---
[1] http://leanpub.com/LoRD

Visit http://makingbrowsergames.com/starterkits/ and try them yourself.

1. Lesson: Game Mechanics

A Dating & Quiz (or sometimes called trivia) game mechanics is a simple "drop-n-drag" or "click & point" designed for non-competitive entertainment or competitive Multi-Player — see example: Get Tiffany Game[1]. A Quiz & Trivia game mechanics seems simple enough; you ask questions and match the gamers' answers *to your defined "correct answers"*. The problem with "Trivia" games is that the information on the Internet doubles every 35 days! You'll become hard pressed to "Keep questions up to date". This is why many Quiz & Trivia games are based on historical information = you can't change what's already happened. If you make the trivia questions too simple, no one will play. Right? Tell me honestly; does anyone really play those trivia games at the restaurant tables while waiting for their waiter/waitress??? I thought so! So, let's not make those same mistakes. But for the "die-hards" that truly want to soak restaurant clients that extra $1.99, I'll include those trivia mechanisms below. In addition, the Internet media has "trained" everyone to expect quizzes to be fairly interactive. So, there's no place for long lists of radio-button, multiple choice quizzes for us.

Quiz & Trivia game mechanics is a sub-genre of the Puzzle game mechanics and education. The gamer is "tested" in their knowledge either through the current gaming session or life experiences. So our game will:

- ask questions in the gamers' native language — so, we'll need to build a large pool of these questions (database?) in each language we want to target. And will we randomly select questions or pose the same questions in the same order each time? Where should we keep the question pool = Locally on the gamer's device or remotely in the cloud? And in what format will we store questions and answers?
- collect input = simple enough, but what style ... text, checkboxes, radio buttons?
- evaluate if the input matches our correct answer,
- record results and display successful progress. Do we even care if the gamer cheats?

---

[1] http://www.gettiffany.com/

All this sounds fairly boring. One of the resource assets in Quiz & Trivia games is the questions in the appropriate language for the gamer. If handled correctly, another option we could follow is tailoring a simple Quiz & Trivia game into an Educational game —teaching the gamer different languages similar to Berlitz Language Center,[2] or Rosetta Stone.[3] For this option, we must know the gamer's native language and which language they want to study. *Quiz & Trivia game fit nicely into the educational genre*.

Dating Sims[2]

by Celso Riva an indie game developer operating Winter Wolves website.[3]

Visual novels are a graphic novel of sorts and a story with optional paths the reader can follow. *Dating sims are very similar in that the reader chooses from on-screen options but the purpose is to develop skills and personal relationships with ingame characters*. These games can have rather complex paths with multiple endings.

To be clear, *they originated in Japan* and, while many visual novels or dating sims are erotic (or at least sexy) in nature, it's not true that all dating sims have erotic content.

It's really a shame that people automatically label these games as "adult only" because, in many cases, is not true. In the case of indie developers, few include racy themes or art as they are often *trying to appeal a more family-friendly audience*.

With this information, let's "spice up"[4] our quiz game and create something that is quite stimulating that will mimic real life — a *"PG-rated"* Dating game[5]! "Say what!?", I hear your thinking. A dating simulation would involve asking and answer questions; what a perfect setting for a Quiz & Trivia game. But how do we know which questions to create? I recommend learning what to ask from the "best" = Neil Strauss as he "picks up" on Jessica Alba[6] or refer to his books "The Rules of the Game — master the art of attraction in 30 days[7]" or "The Game: Penetrating the Secret Society of

---

[2] https://www.gamasutra.com/blogs/CelsoRiva/20150713/248338/Making_and_selling_visual_novels_and_dating_sims.php
[3] https://www.winterwolves.com/
[4] https://idioms.thefreedictionary.com/spice+up
[5] https://en.wikipedia.org/wiki/The_Dating_Game
[6] https://www.youtube.com/watch?v=hC0hrqbhx5M
[7] http://amzn.to/2zQmN7a

Pickup Artists[8]". These books should provide plenty of information to create our dating simulation with questions and answers.

Search the Internet for "dating simulation games" and you will find literally billions of hits. Wikipedia provides some confusion as to what a dating simulation genre is all about. They state[9]:

> **Dating sims**, or **relationship simulation role-playing games (RS-RPG)**, are a video game subgenre[10] of simulation games[11], usually Japanese, with romantic elements. They are also sometimes put under the category of neo-romance. The most common objective of dating sims is to date, usually choosing from among several characters, and to achieve a romantic relationship.
>
> The term "dating sim" is also often used incorrectly in English as a generic term for romance-driven games (ren'ai games), a subject matter which is stereotypically associated with the visual novel[12] genre. This can lead to confusion, as visual novels[13] are considered a subgenre of adventure games[14] and are not technically included in the dating sim genre. While the two genres often share a common visual presentation, dating sims are sometimes considered to be more statistically based than the "choose your own adventure[15]" style of visual novels.
>
> The technical definition of a dating simulation game, known as a romantic simulation game (XXXXXXXXXXX ren'ai shimyurēshon gēmu) in Japan, can involve several technical elements such as a time limit, several statistics such as looks and charm which can be boosted through exercise, or an "attraction meter" which can increase or decrease depending on one's decisions.

In their dance to describe a "romance" game, Wikipedia never states how to deliver such a game nor do they mention the fundamental game mechanics required.

---

[8]http://amzn.to/2BX2CXo
[9]https://en.wikipedia.org/wiki/Dating_sim
[10]https://en.wikipedia.org/wiki/Video_game_genres
[11]https://en.wikipedia.org/wiki/Simulation_video_game
[12]https://en.wikipedia.org/wiki/Visual_novel
[13]https://en.wikipedia.org/wiki/Visual_novel
[14]https://en.wikipedia.org/wiki/Adventure_game
[15]https://en.wikipedia.org/wiki/Interactive_fiction

Simply stated, dating sims and romance games are nothing more than question and answer quizzes.

Game Features

Quiz & Trivia games typically have the following mechanisms and game mechanics:

- Interactive fiction and story plot to provide the background settings.

- A storage system.

- Recursive logic for question validation.

- Tile click/hit detection.

- Timers and delay events.

- Arcade physics if images and sprites (buttons) are used.

- Scoring, awards, hints, and other informational text displays in the gamer's native language.

- Artificial Intelligence (AI) assistant to tutor oversights as hard to find matches or as an antagonist player. Perhaps a chatbot?

Homework & Research:

- Visual Novel ideas - Ren'Py https://www.renpy.org/ latest.html

- http://en.wikipedia.org/wiki/Dating_sim

- (Distribution Channel) https://store.steampowered.com/tags/en/Dating+Sim

- (Distribution Channel) https://itch.io/games/tag-dating-sim

- http://arianeb.com/dategame.htm

Dating Resources

- Exactly what to say in a first message[16]

- 10 Simple Mistakes Men make in online Dating[17]

---

[16] https://theblog.okcupid.com/exactly-what-to-say-in-a-first-message-2bf680806c72
[17] https://www.eharmony.com/blog/10-simple-mistakes-men-make-online-dating/#.WzuJttJKiUk

Exercise Lesson 1:

Take this exercise online[18]

Marketing Exercise — Search the Internet for the phrase "dating simulation games". Record items that:

- have interesting descriptions. Why?
- have illustrations that capture your attention. Why?
- are these games Single— or Multi—Player? Why?

Lesson 1 Quiz:

Take this quiz online[19]

---
[18] http://leanpub.com/courses/leanpub/mbg-dating/quizzes/exercise1
[19] http://leanpub.com/courses/leanpub/mbg-dating/quizzes/lesson1-1

… offers several unique demonstrations and examples of the trivia/quiz game mechanics as a "Dating Sims". Many appeal to raw passion to encourage gamers to return; you've been warned:

- Dating Sims[1] short article listing 100s of sims.
- Newgrounds.com[2] — demos are mostly Flash ActionScript game.
- Games2win.com[3] — demos on "forbidden kissing"[4] and "naughty games"[5] launched their success. Try their Speed Dating 2 here.[6]
- Sim Girls[7] (one of the oldest running romance game series) and the author's newest series BlackSpears[8] combines dress-up fashion and RPG game mechanics. Visit their website here.[9]
- http://ninasays.so/datingsim/ (worth the time to study!)

Game Tools & Generators

You will discover many supporting tools from GitHub and the Appendix in this book. There are tools that will help in the generating gaming ideas.

Random Game Mechanics Generator[10] — This idea generation machine randomly selects 3 — by default — common game theory mechanics. The game mechanics and descriptions should help your

---

[1] https://tvtropes.org/pmwiki/pmwiki.php/Main/DatingSim
[2] https://www.newgrounds.com/games/browse/genre/simulation-dating
[3] http://amzn.to/2EimbL3
[4] http://www.games2win.com/en/romance-games.asp
[5] http://www.games2win.com/en/naughty-games.asp
[6] http://www.games2win.com/en/romance-games/speed-dating-2-game.asp
[7] https://www.newgrounds.com/portal/view/594476
[8] http://www.blackspears.com/index.html
[9] http://simdatinggames.com/dating-sims-for-guys/
[10] http://makingbrowsergames.com/gameDesigner/index-randommechanic.html

Lesson: Game Examples & Research

imagination blend and produce the next blockbuster game.

Game Mechanisms[11] — This library of game controls and mechanism spans several JavaScript gaming frameworks. (more are on the way!) This tool helps you choose the game controls then opens the generic code snapshots (aka snippets). Spend a minute to re-factor the snapshots to your design and you have a functional game prototype in minutes.

This tutorial website offers several unique demonstrations and examples:

- Quiz & Trivia with RPG Adventure integration[12] — demo and transpiled from our 2011 released Flash ActionScript game. I offer three sample Dating and Triva games, and a look at other popular trivia samples

Homework & Research:

- **Highly recommended reading**: So You Want To / **Write a Dating Sim**[13] an article with advice, settings, plot devices, pitfalls to avoid, target audience analysis, suggested themes and motifs, blockbusting game successes and failures.
- Read Romance Side Quest[14] article and collect ideas for your game production by using romance enhanced side quest in other game genres.

Exercise 2: Develop a Unique Game

Take this exercise online[15]

Research: Record your thoughts in an external Journal for future reference. Submission is not required to continue the course.

Write down 3 things you like about the dating sims and games demonstrations.

Write down 3 things you would change, add, or modify.

---

[11]http://makingbrowsergames.com/gameDesigner/index-controlMechanisms.html
[12]http://makingbrowsergames.com/starterkits/quiz/
[13]https://tvtropes.org/pmwiki/pmwiki.php/SoYouWantTo/WriteADatingSim
[14]https://tvtropes.org/pmwiki/pmwiki.php/Main/RomanceSidequest
[15]http://leanpub.com/courses/leanpub/mbg-dating/quizzes/exercise2

Lesson 2 Quiz:

[Take this quiz online](http://leanpub.com/courses/leanpub/mbg-dating/quizzes/lesson2)

3. Lesson: Game Flow

When a gamer launches our featured game from the `index.html` page, we lead them through a series of *menu screens or game phases*. Eventually, they will click a "play" button somewhere on the "main menu" to start the "Game Loop". Download the Game Flowchart from

http://makingbrowsergames.com/starterkits/_GameFlowChart.pdf

Each screen has "its own internal essential functions".[1] These phases give a way to organize our code into modules and ensure that only the minimal game assets (for this current phase) are supplied at just the proper time. These "game scene modules" help us isolate distinct phases from each other. For example, booting the game; loading assets; main menu; playing level one, two, winning, losing, etc. *This is an important concept since game scenes in Phaser v3 are more autonomous*. The goal we achieve, by using this "finite state machine (FMS)" structure, makes our game development simpler and less painful to support.

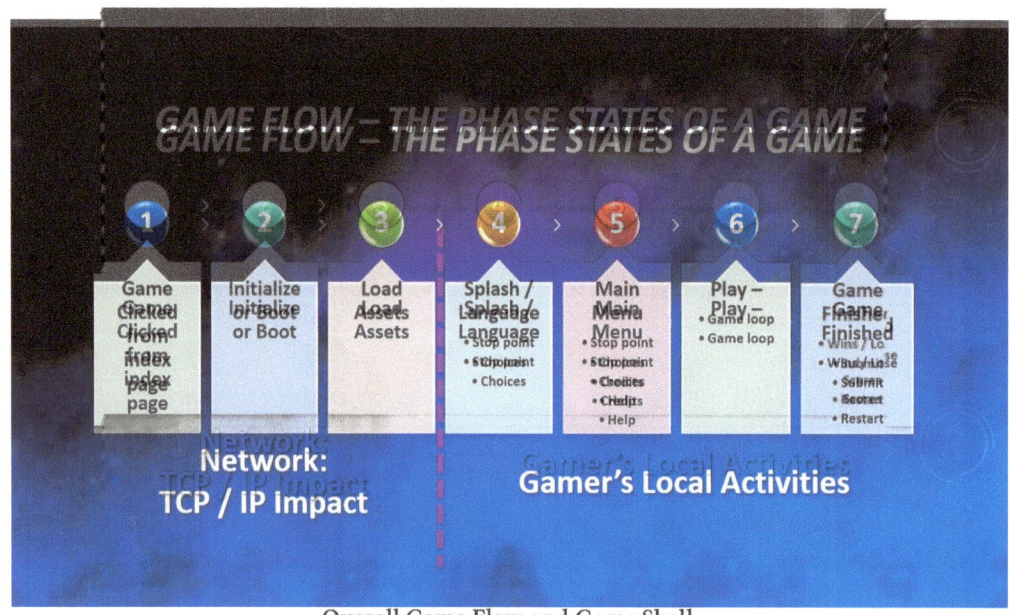

Overall Game Flow and Game Shell

Network Impact

Let's review the first three typical states *after the `index.html` page: boot, preload, and splash scenes*. In practice, your gamers would see a progress bar then after a few seconds, the first "splash" or "language selection" menu. The network has the most impact on our game during these initial phases.

Placing our game as close to the player will help their perception of how quick and lively our game is. "How do we ensure our game deployment is close to our consumers?", you say. By *[using a content delivery network!][1]* The sample `index.html` source code offers two choices to pull the Phaser framework from a content delivery network. Once your game reaches the "splash/language" scene, all activity is on the gamers' device as a "single-player" game. You'll find the following phrase, "Stop point" in illustration below. What I mean is these are excellent times to load additional game assets. Your game has met the "App Stores" requirements on activation within 20 seconds; now, while the gamer is considering various choices you offered, is the perfect time *to turn on web sockets or download further assets in the background*.

Each of these phases is governed internally by the "Essential" Phaser functions (listed below). Each Game Screen's responsibility is to control the flow of each game flow phases. Each of these "Essential Phaser Functions" is included in every scene.

- The "Initiate or Boot"[2] phase sets-up current variables, canvas dimensions, browser orientation, and data for this specific scene.
- The "preload"[3] phase manages the game assets, downloading, and storing them in each unique Phaser Cache.
- The "create" phase makes the loaded game assets available.
- The "update" phase attempts to collect the "whereabouts" of all the game assets on the stage (aka camera view) at approximately 60 frames per second (fps). In Phaser v3, you now have the option to manage the fps using the Tween Manager.
- The "render" phase publishes the new game asset positions. In Phaser v3, you now have a choice

---
[1] https://www.cdnperf.com/

of "Dynamic" or "Static" rendering.

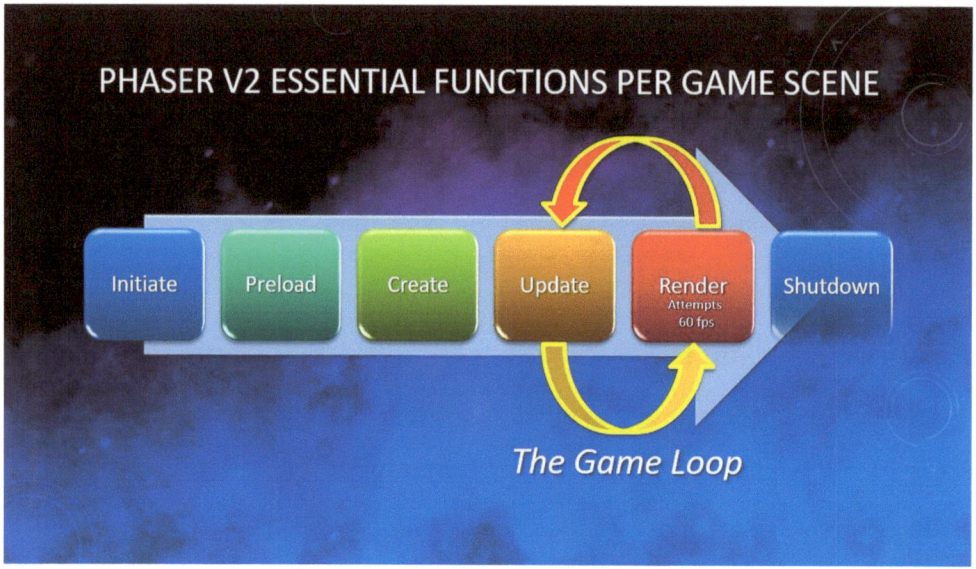

Figure: Phaser Essential Functions

The Game loop's responsibility, illustrated above, is to control the flow of several game elements. The Game Loop is the standard "universal process" of **input, process, and output**. It re-cycles until the game migrates to a new phase. The Phaser v2 game loop has many moving parts inside, and the render phase attempts to maintain a rate of 60 times per second.

There's an interesting twist in our sample games we provide at this books website. In the Shibuya-gyaru demonstration[2], the gamer is asked questions and is also able to present questions – a tit for tat[3] situation. We will generate a simple artificial intelligence to determine when to ask or answer a question.

---

[2]http://makingbrowsergames.com/starterkits/quiz/Shibuya-gyaru.html
[3]https://dictionary.cambridge.org/us/dictionary/english/tit-for-tat

Lesson: Game Flow

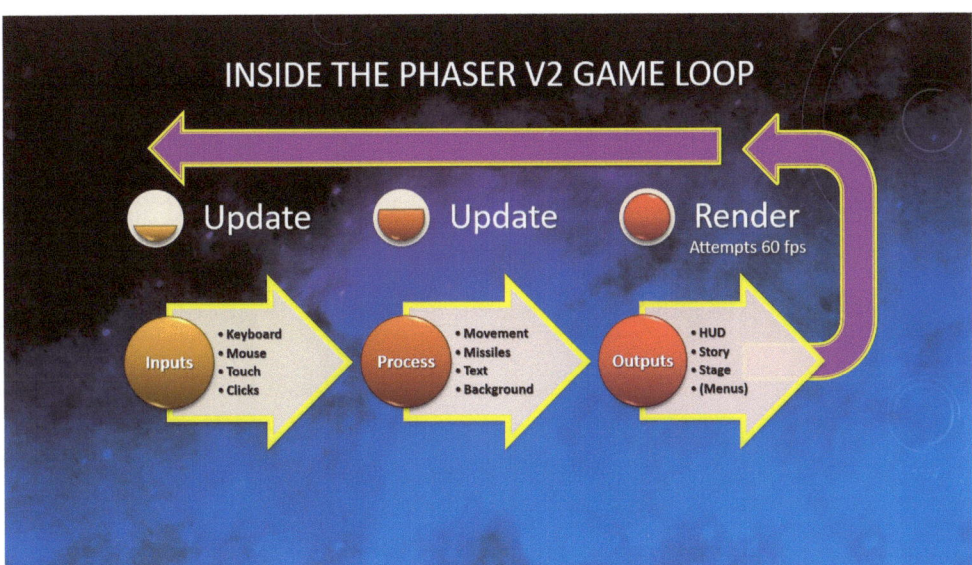

Figure: Phaser v2 Game Loop

Let's write some more code. Here's what our *Phaser v2 game skeleton framework* looks like. The following code is generic style across all Phaser v2 games; it is called "game.js" (or "main.js"). This will be our standard game creation template **for Phaser v2** called "game Skeleton". Phaser 3 is extremely flexible and adds several innovative ways to achieve this similar "game set-up".

Our game is a simple JavaScript Object resting inside the Browser Object Model (BOM) "window".[4] W3Schools states, "The Browser Object Model (BOM) allows JavaScript to "talk to" the browser. … There are no official standards for the **B**rowser **O**bject **M**odel (BOM). … The **window** object is supported by all browsers. It represents the browser's window. All global JavaScript objects, functions, and variables automatically become members of the window object."[5]

Note: This example is available as a bonus content download from http://makingbrowsergames.com/starterkits/_v2gameSkeletonJS.pdf

- Reference 1, we "use strict"[6] to avoid fat-fingering, nasty bugs, poor assignments and the like. Comments are our friend. Use them generously! Console logging is our best friend and worth the investigation to use properly.[7]

- Reference 2: Let's declare the global application object or "namespace". This creates our JavaScript

Lesson: Game Flow

game (object) = the "constructor", and inside we set the game's dimensions to the Golden ratio[8]. Our Phaser game will live inside this JavaScript object and is protected from memory collisions; this is a "namespace technique".[9] Also, our game states (the various phases and menus a gamer would migrate through to play our game) will be kept safely in this global object.[10] This article is an excellent primer for the new Phaser v3 namespaces and game scenes.[11] The suggests here are not the only way to create JavaScript namespaces; this is one of the hardest concepts for those new to the Phaser Game Framework. Trying to understand why Phaser games look so different is best explained by this side-trip article.[12]

- Reference 3: extends our newly created "Game" object with a prototype inheritance chain. This attaches all our internal game functions to our newly created object above.
- Reference 4: our preload game assets. Remember the game must be active within 20 seconds or we stand rejection from the "app stores".
- Reference 5: create links our newly downloaded assets into the game.
- Reference 6: update will continually read the inputs and modifications and render the results to the gamer.
- Reference 7: render is reserved for new information after the displayed updates and debug information.
- Reference 8: Ties the Phaser Game Engine and framework into a variable for our DOM canvas tag.
- Reference 9: are a glimpse into what's new in the upcoming Phaser v3 – to quote Dorothy from the Wizard of Oz, "We're not in Kansas anymore!"

Excerise 3: Network Research

Take this exercise online[4]

Research: Record your thoughts on what might delay or corrupt your game across the Wide Area Network (i.e.: telephone network, cell phone network.) Submission is not required to continue the course.

---

[4]http://leanpub.com/courses/leanpub/mbg-dating/quizzes/exercise3

Write down 3 things you believe might delay your games across a Wide Area network.

Research Content Delivery Networks (click here)[5]. Who is the fastest?

Test Content Delivery Networks (click here)[6] for world-wide access and delay.

Lesson 3 Quiz:

Take this quiz online[7]

Notes

1 Gose, S. (2016, July 24). Phaser Game Prototyping. Retrieved August 20, 2017, from https://leanpub.com/LoRD

2 http://makingbrowsergames.com/starterkits/quiz/v2_quiz_game2_bootJS.pdf

3 http://makingbrowsergames.com/starterkits/quiz/v2_quiz_game2_loadJS.pdf

4 https://www.quora.com/What-is-a-browser-window

5 https://www.w3schools.com/js/js_window.asp

6 https://stackoverflow.com/questions/1335851/what-does-use-strict-do-in-javascript-and-what-is-the-reasoning-behind-it

7 https://developers.google.com/web/tools/chrome-devtools/console/

8 https://www.goldennumber.net/

9 http://lucybain.com/blog/2015/js-namespacing/

10 https://www.codeproject.com/Articles/829254/JavaScript-Namespace

11 https://javascriptweblog.wordpress.com/2010/12/07/namespacing-in-javascript/

12 https://www.safaribooksonline.com/library/view/learning-javascript-design/9781449334840/ch13s15.html

---

[5] https://www.cdnperf.com/
[6] https://www.cdnperf.com/tools/cdn-latency-benchmark
[7] http://leanpub.com/courses/leanpub/mbg-dating/quizzes/lesson3

II Starting a Dating | Quiz Game Project

Enough chit-chat, let's dive into some code-filing structures. You could create this project's file structure by creating each directory manually; OR, you could use Yeoman and generate your *Phaser project automatically*[8]. If that seems too intimidating, then your best alternative is to *download our FREE Phaser Game Prototype template*[9] which follows our instructions in this document. Our project directory structure follows the Phaser Game Prototype workbook examples found at

http://makingbrowsergames.com/book/

Project Files and Directories

At a minimum, we need two files and two directory folders:

1. An index.html file that launches our game,
2. A `Main.js` file[13] — name it anything you'd like — found inside the newly created JavaScript ("js") directory folder; and finally
3. An assets directory folder in which we'll store all our game graphics, sounds, question text, and images.

---

[8]https://www.npmjs.com/package/generator-yo-phaser
[9]http://makingbrowsergames.com/starterkits/

These are part of the Bonus Content downloads at
http://makingbrowsergames.com/starterkits/

The benefits gained from using either Yeoman or our FREE Game Prototype template is that all your projects will have a consistent "look and feel" during construction. That means faster, quicker game creation and deployments. It becomes a simple matter to generate a game every 30- or even 7-days! Imagine this within one year from now, you could have 12 to 52 games in the "Apps Stores".

```
.(top root directory - single player)
├── favicon.ico
├── index.html
├── license.txt
├── manifest.json
├── package.json        //for Progressive Web Applications
├── purchaseOrder.pdf
├── ReadMe.md
│
├── assets
│   ├── audio
│   ├── images
│   └── spriteSheets
│
├── css
│   └── main.css
├── fonts
│   └── fonts.css
│
└── js
    ├── libraries
    ├── plugins
    ├── prefabs
    ├── states
    └── utilities
```

I label "assets" as the place to hold all game images, sprites, and sounds — since I am the original creator of them, and they are copyrightable[14]. Let's not worry about putting any of these items in the "asset directory folders" for now. We'll do that later — after we have our source code drafted and operational. Here's what another famous game developer says:

"Challenge yourself to create a code-base that compiles and runs in the first few hours. Make it so that you can accept inputs, move around, animate something, and trigger some sounds. This prototype, lousy a game as it may be, is going to be your best friend. The sooner you can have a working early playable prototype, the more likely you are to succeed.

No-art prototypes also have one other major advantage: in previous games, I would make beautiful mock-ups in PhotoShop and gather hundreds of lovely looking sprites in preparation for the game. After development was complete, the vast majority of the art had to be replaced, re-sized, or thrown out. I've wasted thousands of hours making game-ready artwork before coding; these days I know that the tech specs and evolving game-play mechanics will mean that much of what you make at the start won't make it into the finished game."[15] by Christer Kaitila: The Chunky-pants Method

 Tip: These are part of the Bonus Content downloads at http://makingbrowsergames.com/starterkits/quiz/ You can review more game mechanics at our supporting website = http://makingbrowsergames.com/starterkits/

Our largest game asset will be our pool of questions and answers.

One last step in our project set-up is getting our index.html page to work properly. There are several ways to do this: If you already have XAMPP[16] (WAMP[17], or LAMPP[18]) installed per Phaser.io's recommendations[19], then we're good to go. If not? Well, I recommend using the **Brackets editor**[20]; it magically runs the required web services for you.

These are the general exercise steps we will follow as we build our game project:

Step 0: Preparation. This is the fun part of development; so, have a party and enjoy!

- **Research and** play similar gaming ideas currently on the market.
- **Write your ideas down or use the** Game Generation Tools above
- **Build your W**orkstation and File Structure.

Step 1: Create your game's index file. Always use "responsive design," and determine whether you want a "standard", "Single Web Page Application"[10] or Progressive Web App (PWA)[11] deployment.

Step 2: Create your game shell scenes as "Standalone" or Content Management System (CMS).

Step 3: Create your game core functions and play scene.

Step 0: Review these demonstrations:

- http://makingbrowsergames.com/starterkits/quiz/
- Other examples are on this course's website[12] ...

Step 1. Create our standard index file:

Let's create two distinctive "front-door delivery systems" for our games. The first delivery version is through a standard index.html web page, and the second version is tailored for mobile devices as a "single web page application" (SWPA)[13] or Progressive Web App (PWA).[14] I recommend using a "mobile first, responsive design" HTML page for all.

We'll begin working on our game's "standard front door" — the index.html file. Create or download it. This file must be labeled "index.html"; this is, unfortunately, NOT a choice in our game development.

 If you're curious as to why? I recommend a side-trip to this article on "Why is it important that we name the main file index.html?"[15]

---

[10] https://www.seguetech.com/what-is-a-single-page-application/
[11] https://developers.google.com/web/progressive-web-apps/
[12] http://makingbrowsergames.com/starterkits/quiz/
[13] https://en.wikipedia.org/wiki/Single-page_application
[14] https://developers.google.com/web/progressive-web-apps/
[15] https://teamtreehouse.com/community/why-is-it-important-that-we-name-the-main-file-indexhtml

Standard HTML5 Index page

```
1   <!doctype html>
2   <html lang="en">
3   <head>
4           <meta charset="UTF-8" />
5           <title>Phaser Game Prototyping - (Your Game Title Here) </title>
6           <meta name="description" content="Phaser Game Prototyping Template" />
7           <link rel="shortcut icon" href="favicon.ico" type="image/x-icon" />
8           <style>
9                   body {margin:0; padding:0; background: #000;}
10                  canvas {margin: 0 auto;}
11          </style>
12          <link rel="stylesheet" type="text/css" href="fonts/fonts.css" />
13          <link rel="stylesheet" type="text/css" href="css/main.css" />
14          <link rel="icon" href="assets/launcher.png" type="image/png" />
15          <link rel="manifest" href="manifest.json" />
16          <!--
17          <script src="https://cdnjs.cloudflare.com/ajax/libs/phaser-ce/2.10.6/phaser.min.js"\
18  ></script>
19          OR
20          <script src="js/phaser3.10.4.min.js"></script>
21          -->
22          <script src="https://cdn.jsdelivr.net/phaser/2.6.2/phaser.min.js"></script>
23          <script defer src="js/main.js"></script>
24
25          <script defer src="js/state/boot.js"></script>
26          <script defer src="js/state/credits.js"></script>
27          <script defer src="js/state/demo.js"></script>
28          <script defer src="js/state/load.js"></script>
29          <script defer src="js/state/menu.js"></script>
30          <script defer src="js/state/play.js"></script>
31
32  </head>
33  <body itemscope itemtype="http://schema.org/CreativeWork/WebApplication">
34          <div id="orientation"></div>
35          <!--
36          NOTE: Phaser library must be loaded prior to any game logic.
37          We load script files here to avoid window.onload call.
38          Window.onload is rarely used for many reasons, and because
39                  Phaser doesn't wait until all resources are loaded.
40          The DOMContentLoaded event triggers when the page is ready.
41          It waits for the full HTML and scripts and then starts.
42          This is explained in greater detail in
```

```
43                    "Phaser.JS Design Guide workbook".
44             NOTE: per the Phaser.JS Design Guide workbook, you may place the following
45             script externally or as the last head script using defer.
46             -->
47
48   </body>
49   </html>
```

 This example is available as a bonus content download from http://makingbrowsergames. com/starterkits/_indexHTML5.pdf.

I prefer loading the game directly into the document.body. Other game developers load their games into a parent <div> tag as a container. It's your choice. Which is best? Take a side-trip to this answer from Adobe[21]. W3Schools.com provides this warning concerning <div> tags saying, "**Note: By default, browsers always place a line break before and after the <div> element. However, this can be changed with CSS.**"[22]

Did you notice how many JavaScript files we're using for our game? During development, this is "ok" and gives you the chance to quickly find those pesky software bugs. The downside is the added time to download and execute each JavaScript file. That's the reason I use "defer" inside the script tags. To compensate for the individual downloads, many developers will use Browserify to create one huge, monolithic, compressed file.

Notice you do not need to change any of its content! This is because we created this initial "front door into our game" in a standard generic format that applies to any game creation within this series. Software engineers call this ***D.R.Y. (Don't Repeat Yourself)*** coding; it saves your time by creating things once and re-using them; it's a ***"building block style" or black-box development***. I said this before, *"Imagine within one year from now, you could have 12 to 52 games in the "Apps Stores"; the secret is keeping your code D.R.Y!*

Mobile Single Web Page Applications

Now for the tailored mobile device index page. This construction is different than before; my goal is to load as much as possible into the single page without exceeding 20 seconds. I have two different styles of mobile device pages. The example below creates a normal JavaScript link to the main.js (or game.js). I take a "less formal" approach in the mobile versions and try to "in-line" scripts inside the index.html's `<div>` tags. **The single web page application** is divided into `<div>` sections. Each `<div>` section represents a single scene and the game.js is placed into the "play game" `<div>`. If the game is small, I will simply insert the entire raw game.js contents directly into a script tag and thus avoid an additional file to download. Do so, ensures the game content is a part of the index.html page.

Single Web Page Application

```
1   <!doctype html>
2   <html lang="en">
3   <head> : : : :
4   </head>
5   <body> : : : :
6
7   <!-- Mobile Dress-UP game -->
8   <div class="ui-content" data-theme="b" data-role="page" id="game">
9       <div data-role="header">
10          <h1><b>(Your Game Title here)</b></h1>
11          <a href=" " class="ui-btn ui-mini ui-icon-home ui-btn-icon-left ">Home</a>
12      </div>
13
14      <div id="game-area" data-role="main" class="ui-content">
15      </div>
16
17      <script src="game.js"></script>
18
19      <div class="ui-content center footer" data-role="footer">
20          <hr class="center" style="width: 60%" />
21          <nav class="menu"><a href='http://www.copyright.gov/fls/fl108.pdf' target='_blank'>\
22          &copy; 1978-2016, <a class="w3-btn btn-footer w3-hover-deep-orange w\
23          3-theme-d3 w3-round-xlarge w3-border w3-text-shadow " href='http://www.stephen-gose.\
24          com/en/' target='_blank'> Stephen Gose LLC </a>. <br />All Rights Reserved. <br />Qu\
25          estions or comments? <a class="w3-btn btn-footer w3-hover-deep-orange w3-theme-d3 w3\
26          -round-xlarge w3-border w3-text-shadow " href="http://www.stephen-gose.com/about/con\
27          tact/"> Please Contact </a><br />
28          <hr class="center" style="width: 60%" />
29          </nav>
30      </div>
```

```
31    </div>
32    <!-- End Game Page -->
```

You can review it at:

http://makingbrowsergames.com/starterkits/quiz/game3/index.html

and as a "*single web page application*" at

http://makingbrowsergames.com/starterkits/quiz/game3/index-mobile-SWPA.html

Sometimes, I like everything in one place; it depends on the size of the game I plan to deploy. All that remains is a method to bind all these into a single web page application (SWPA)[16]. Using a single monolithic file has advantages per Google's new(?) Accelerated Mobile Pages Project (AMP)[17]. We'll do this through our game's index.html page. Many authors create yet another script file, but I prefer to use an inline scripting for mobile devices.

Excellent work! Our game page is ready to use and load our game. Creating our Quiz & Trivia source code would be our next "step"; but, let's review how our game works.

https://learntocodewith.me/programming/basics/text-editors/

Step 2. Create your standard game scenes:

Return to the Introduction section and review the Game Phases.

Choose whether we are creating a standard or mobile game. Then if you chose a mobile game, you should determine whether you want *a mobile "single web page application" (SWPA)* or a more traditional structure. The *single web page application* contains everything inside its `index.html` page. The `game.js` becomes a script tag inside one of the `<div>` tags as we discussed earlier. This will determine where the Main.js will reside. The earlier examples all used a "mobile first" responsive design in the `index.html`.

---

[16] https://www.seguetech.com/what-is-a-single-page-application/
[17] https://www.ampproject.org/

Let's create all the supporting game phases as separate JavaScript files. They all follow the generic format found in the Introduction Section: Phaser v2 Game Flow We'll place these files inside the /js/states/directory. Only a few changes are needed in the following files for this game genre:

- Main.js — which holds all the configuration characteristics and supporting functions of our games.

- Boot.js — designates our game assets to download. If we maintain the "naming convention", we simply have to create new artwork with the same file names found in the boot.js file and add any new items.

- MainMenu.js — perhaps small tweaks to our for unique options for this specific game?

- Play.js — which would normally be our game's loop; however, we will combine the play scene into the mainMenu scene. It will make perfect sense if you study the example on http://makingbrowsergames.com/starterkits/quiz/v2.6.2/index.html

 Press "F12" to watch the "behind the scenes" activities.

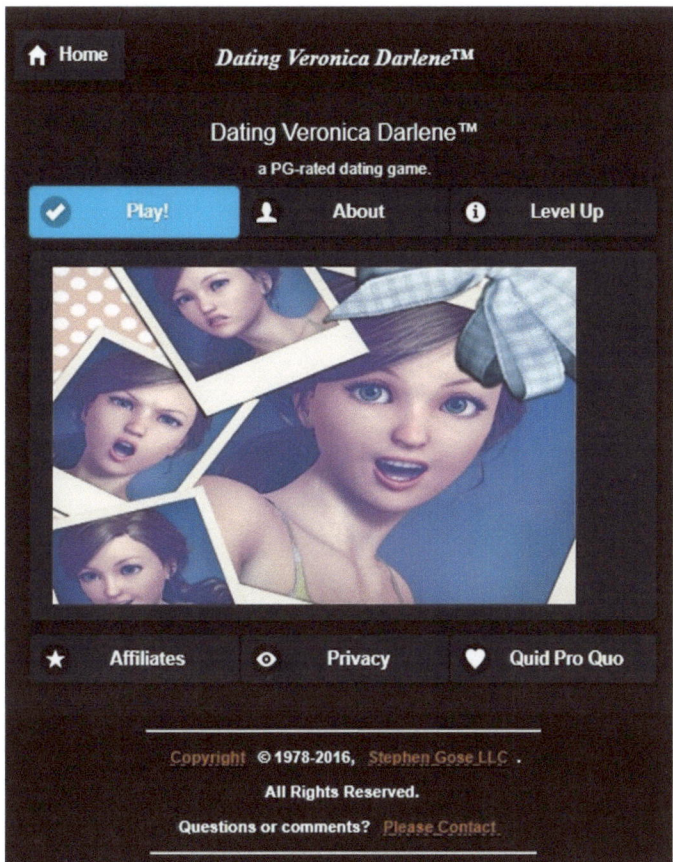

Mobile version with theme

Core Game Phases

We will create two distinctive delivery styles of Dating & Quiz games; one for normal web browser and the following tailored for a mobile device.

Main.js

This JavaScript file "IS" the game. It holds all the configuration logic used during the play phase. What you entitle this file is not critical, but always name it the same across all your projects. Why? Because we have a "D.R.Y." thing going on and we want "stay dry" — to keep our consistency across all our development projects. There's another reason: NAMESPACE SECURITY! As players launch and play our collection of games, one game will "over-write" another.

This file also holds our initial language text to prompt the player's selection. We use their selection to trigger a JSON language file.

 NOTE: You can download this file from *http://makingbrowsergames.com/starterkits/quiz/v2_quiz_game2_mainJS.pdf* Review this file; it is thoroughly annotated and documented to reduce the price of this pamphlet.

Boot.js

This game phase has the responsibility of configuring and setting-up the html5 canvas, keyboard, and game physics. As the name suggests, its purpose prepares the web browser and sets the game dimensions = loading various game assets and storing them in Phaser v2 cache, having them readily available when needed throughout the game. Once the canvas is prepared, it will typically hand-off control toward the next phase called the "load" phase. Since this file is typically small, I sometimes "in line" the script inside the index.html page to avoid the added download time. This is especially important for mobile games. Here's an article that discusses the advantages and disadvantages.[18] Once again, it's your choice.

The pool of questions will be our largest game asset, but at this point, we do not know the gamer's language. Yes, we could guess their language from their IP address, but that's not 100% certain. What if they are vacationing in Singapore or Tokyo? We will delay downloading the question pool until the right time.

Some game developers take a "more formal" approach and split each internal game phase into distinct classifications or module files (for example missiles.js, avatar.js, enemyShips.js, gameHandler.js, ad nauseum). They do this for several reasons

- during development to easily find and squash those nasty software bugs.

- To maintain "separation of concerns".[19]

---

[18] https://softwareengineering.stackexchange.com/questions/86589/why-should-i-avoid-inline-scripting
[19] https://en.wikipedia.org/wiki/Separation_of_concerns

Then, when they're ready to release their game, they use various tools to [obfuscate, minify, and re-merge](#)[20] all those separate modules back into a single game file again – just as we have done here already!

In our mobile SWPA demonstration example of **Dating Veronica Darlene**™, we collapsed everything into a single file called 'game.js'. I took a "less formal approach" using a ["single web page application" (SWPA)](#)[21]. Since the SWPA boot.js is so small, I "inlined" it inside the index-swpa.html page to avoid the added download time. Be sure to [read this article](#)[22] that discusses the advantages and disadvantages. Once again, it's your choice. Now let's move on to the preload state.

- init function – prepares critical variables for game usage
- preload function – manages downloaded audio, images, and spriteSheets
- create function – manages the game re-size (min and max), alignment, and input
- enterIncorrectOrientation function – notify gamer
- leaveIncorrectOrientation function – adjust game

NOTE: You can download this file from

http://makingbrowsergames.com/starterkits/quiz/v2_quiz_game2_bootJS.pdf

Review this file; it is thoroughly annotated and documented to reduce the price of this pamphlet. Now let's move on to the preload state.

Preload.js

This Game Phase manages our number of files to download; you should optimize this process with the fewest downloads immediately required by your game. In a normal **CodeIgniter CMS** game, I "inline" the normal boot.js into the index.html and consolidated everything else into a 'game.js'; by doing so, I have deferred several potential downloaded files with this single combined file.

Many developers use [Browserify](#)[23] to the same effect. The formal and separate preload.js now

---

[20] https://medium.freecodecamp.org/javascript-modules-part-2-module-bundling-5020383cf306
[21] https://en.wikipedia.org/wiki/Single-page_application
[22] https://softwareengineering.stackexchange.com/questions/86589/why-should-i-avoid-inline-scripting
[23] http://browserify.io/

becomes a simple JavaScript object in a **single web page application (SWPA)** Illustrated below is the "preload" process inside the "game.js".

Reference	
1	preload function – manages game assets downloads
2	create function – prepares a download bar and progress

NOTE: You can download this file from

http://makingbrowsergames.com/book/index11.htm

http://makingbrowsergames.com/starterkits/quiz/v2_quiz_game2_loadJS.pdf

Review this file; it is thoroughly annotated and documented to reduce the price of this pamphlet.

Example: Preload.js internalized as a JavaScript Object

```
// ============================================================
// --------------------------------------------
// Supporting game Function & Classes
// --------------------------------------------
//**TODO**:
//          Change namespace from generic GAMEAPP to your project
//          refactor and adjust for your game deployment
//          remove console debug information on public deployment
// ============================================================
// act as a Preload.js, preloads graphics and enable scaling
var preloadAssets = function(game){};

preloadAssets.prototype = {
        preload: function(){
                game.load.spritesheet("tiles", "assets/sprites/tiles.png", tileSize, tileSize);
                game.load.spritesheet("soundicons", "assets/sprites/soundicons.png", 80, 80);
        },
        create: function(){
                game.stage.backgroundColor = '#252525';
                game.state.start("TitleScreen");
        }
}
```

Splash.js or Language.js

Finally, we should arrive at our splash scene within 20 seconds; if our game takes longer than 20 seconds to activate, it stands rejection from most "app stores". Here is an excellent place to inform our gamers about our sponsorship, provide advertisements, **language selection** and present your branding and logos. While the gamer pauses to select their language, it is an excellent time to download more game assets **or (better yet!) launch your game's web socket connection**.[23] This scene allows another place to download any further assets (e.g.: our game questions), display a progress bar, play mood/theme music and art. A word of caution here, all "app store" require your game to be "live and active" within 20 seconds.

What we will do is present a "language menu" to gamers and let them select — *dynamically on-demand!!* — their native language for continued game-play and interaction. *Phaser Game Design Workbook*[24] covers this topic more thoroughly and provides insight into the most popular languages on the Internet — English is not the fastest growing and is now less than half of the languages represented.

The natural choice is a button mechanism for language selection designed around the gamer's national flag; "iconic symbols" ARE the international language. When a gamer glides over any nation's flag, the tool-tip text changes to that nation's predominant language. Mesmerized by the sudden display of various languages and spellings, and gamers —doing what they do best (i.e.: play) — could spend perhaps 3 whole seconds goofing around, thus providing us time for downloading more game resources *through perhaps a newly activated web socket*. Naturally, there must be a different method to handle mobile touch input. Clever as gamers are, they will select click their native language using their national flag as the visual clue. On that click-event, the internal game functions will send a request to download a JSON language file and dynamically populate (e.g.: substitute) all text variables inside the game. Here are some interesting facts about the Internet and *who your "real" target audience is.*[25]

---

[24]https://leanpub.com/phaserjsgamedesignworkbook
[25]http://www.internetworldstats.com/stats.htm

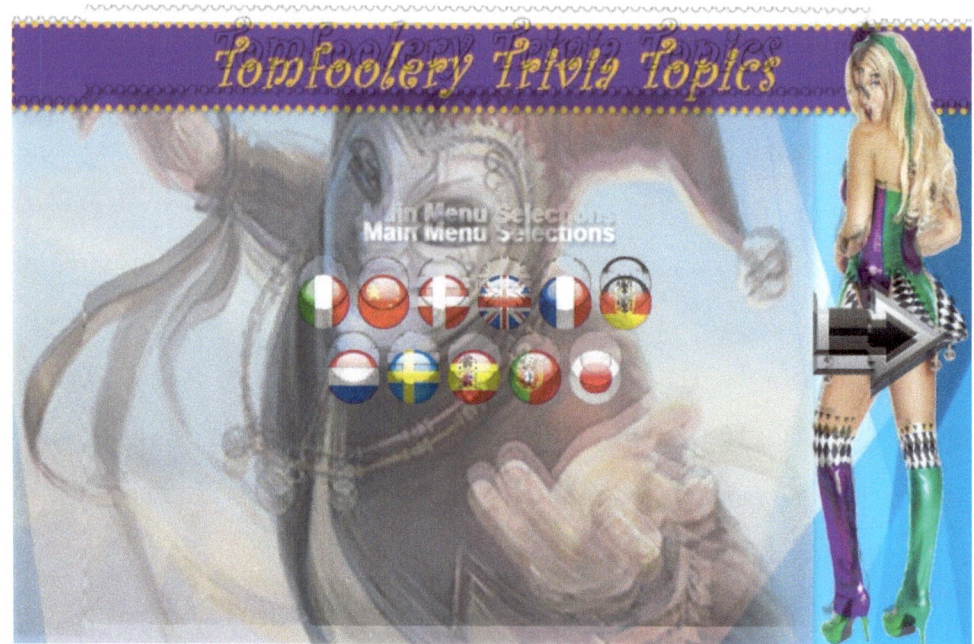

Language Selection

NOTE: You can try a live demonstration from http://makingbrowsergames.com/book/ch3/SCRUM2/index.html and review the source code from http://makingbrowsergames.com/book/index9.html&35;9.4

For our Mobile SWPA, we use another `<div>` tag inside the index.html file. Review the mobile index.html source code, and you find that the "splash scene" is merely a "div" tag using Bootstrap CSS.

Menu.js

Our next screen is the game's main menu. It is during this game scene we now load the language text for all questions and menus. Usually, we divide our game into various levels of difficulty (depending on your game's genre and how you plan to implement it). In the *Phaser Game Design Workbook*[26]; I go into greater depth on workflow, how to load scripts (sync, async or deferred), and the use of internationalization (language selections).

---
[26] https://leanpub.com/phaserjsgamedesignworkbook

On the main menu, you should offer your gamers several options before starting their game's play in earnest. The following scripts could be handled better as separate HTML web pages **in a content management system (CMS)** rather than stuffing everything into a Phaser Canvas. Remember the HTML5 canvas tag is merely a graphical display; it replaces the former Adobe Flash plugin in essence.

Reference	
1	preload function – not used; everything was downloaded in the boot.js
2	create function – links downloaded assets for use during the game.
3	beginGame function – manages theme music
4	gameCredits function – manages theme music and game author information
5	MoreGame function - manages theme music, and provides access to more games from the author

NOTE: You can download this file from

http://makingbrowsergames.com/starterkits/quiz/v2_quiz_game2_menuJS.pdf

The following scripts are not included and would be better handled as separate HTML web pages in a content management system. Visit **other games on the book's website** for examples of a **content management system (CMS)**.

- `About.js` = a page biography to enhance your portfolio and resume. In our mobile demonstration, the 'about page' is used to enhance SEO and page content since it is simply another '<div>' tag.
- `Credits.js` = a page giving attributions.
- `Donations.js` – a page requesting financial support.
- `Instructions.js` or `help.js` – a page offering helpful hints, walk-throughs, achievement, awards, entitlements, or game rules. If the game instructions are minimal in content, it could be combined with another page.
- `Language.js` – a page offering gameplay in their native language.
- `MoreGame.js` – a redirection page to your whole collection of games; used to build a loyal fan base.

Live example at:

http://makingbrowsergames.com/starterkits/memorymatch/v2.6.2-seq/index.html

- `Options.js` – a configuration page used to set keyboard input, and the like. Live example at http://www.adventurers-of-renown.com/quests/arra.php/welcome/lobby.html

- `Scores.js` – pulls from a master database of recorded scores.

- `Share.js` – a page to enhance viral distribution of your game or announcements within the game. See the twitter enhancement[27].

- `SubmitScores.js` – collects and transmits of current game session for permanent storage.

   - wins.js – records information into the gamer's registered account.

   - loose.js – records information into the gamer's registered account.

- `WebMasters.js` – a page offering license and distribution information.

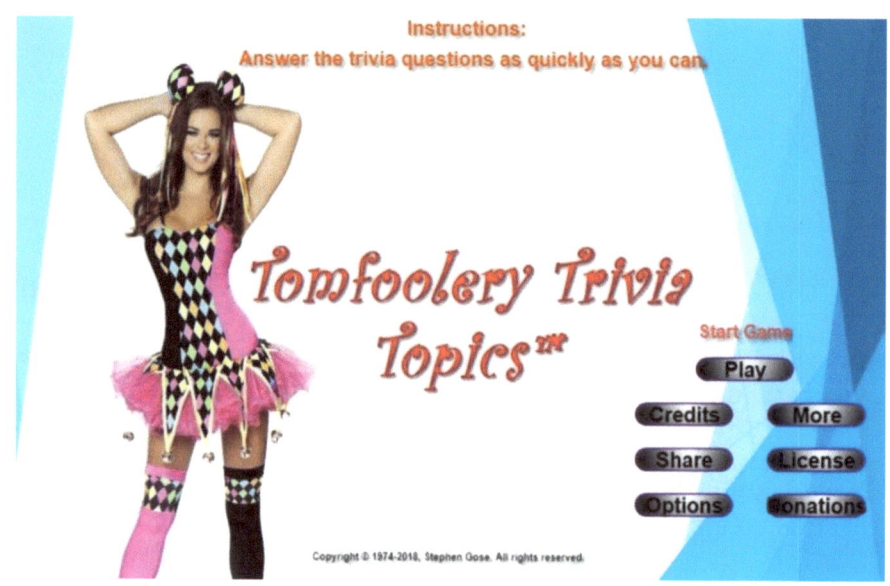

CMS main menu (external)

NOTE: You can download this file from

http://makingbrowsergames.com/starterkits/quiz/v2_quiz_game2_menuJS.pdf

Review this file; it is thoroughly annotated and documented to reduce the price of this pamphlet.

---

[27]http://makingbrowsergames.com/starterkits/_twitterEnhancementJS.pdf

upcoming book: Phaser MMoG development - https://leanpub.com/b/ultimatephaserlibrary#bundle-page-rrgamingsystem

Step 3: Dating | Quiz Games' Logic & Supporting Functions

I have created three different **Quiz & Trivia**. Each of these demonstrates different construction considerations.

Credit Scene as Static Image with Sponsor

NOTE: You can download this file from

http://makingbrowsergames.com/starterkits/quiz/v2_quiz_game2_creditsJS.pdf

http://makingbrowsergames.com/starterkits/quiz/v2_quiz_game2_menuJS.pdf

Review this file; it is thoroughly annotated and documented to reduce the price of this pamphlet.

The first game (#1) dynamically generates a pool of questions and follows a "non-traditional" Phaser construction. Some of its features include

1. dynamically labeled sprint buttons, and extended data;
2. Using the Phaser `update` function as a gaming engine;
3. Creating a Phaser "single-state" game.

The second game (#2) follows the "traditional" Phaser game construction as described in Phaser Game Prototypes[28] and mentioned earlier in this chapter. Some of its features include:

1. importing the question pool from remote sources, and the reason for doing so;
2. dynamically labeled sprint buttons, and extended data;
3. Using the Phaser `update` function as a gaming engine;
4. Creating a Phaser "multi-states in the `playGame` scene;
5. dynamically adjust all text to the gamer's native language.
6. Learning when to create static scenes.

The third game (#3) follows the "traditional" Phaser game construction. Its focus is on using a local database pool download from a remote source. Some of its features include:

1. Using SQLite with Phaser;
2. Using the Phaser `update` function as a gaming engine;
3. dynamically labeled sprint buttons, and extended data;
4. Creating a Phaser "multi-states in the `playGame` scene;
5. dynamically adjust all text to the gamer's native language;
6. Dynamically adjust AI to various personalities played, and environments selected.

---

[28] https://leanpub.com/LoRD

Notes

13 Some developers will name this file the "game.js". It's your decision; but once decided, please stay consistent

14 Now might be a good time to review what the US Copyrights & Patent Office says concerning games and copyrights. Read: https://www.copyright.gov/fls/fl108.pdf

15 #1GAM: How to Succeed at Making One Game a Month. (n.d.). Retrieved August 30, 2017, from https://gamedevelopment.tutsplus.com/articles/1gam-how-to-succeed-at-making-one-game-a-month--gamedev-3695

16 https://www.apachefriends.org/index.html

17 https://bitnami.com/stack/wamp/installer

18 https://wiki.sabayon.org/index.php?title=HOWTO:_Install_LAMPP_/_XAMPP_web_development_environment

19 http://phaser.io/tutorials/getting-started

20 http://brackets.io/

21 DIV tags, and why use them? https://forums.adobe.com/thread/571486

22 https://www.w3schools.com/tags/tag_div.asp

23 More about Web Sockets, SSE, RTMP, and Web RTC thoroughly covered in

III Game #1 – Menza Mental Math™: a math tutor game.

Menza Mental Math™ is a Trade and service mark of Stephen Gose LLC. All rights reserved.

Now let us dive straight into creating the game board, entities, and pieces for a simple math trivia game. This game will present a simple math equation and pose possible answers — **all this from a dynamically generated question pool in the gamer's browser — nothing to download!** Since math and numbers are fairly universal, we'll avoid our standard language-selection menu. Furthermore, this game should follow a "non-traditional" format; it should be a "single-state" and "single web page application" game. But I forced you to read this far into the pamphlet, so let's stick to what we've learned and practiced our newly gained knowledge in the next game's example.

The following functions support the **Quiz & Trivia** game logic and manage user interactions. I have inserted them into the game.js since they are only required during the gameplay phase. I have used simple structural programming, but have grouped functions that could have become classes.

Design Note:

Although game #1 may appear similar to this article[29], it is a complete re-write in JS OLOO (objects linking to other objects; it shuns the classical OOP) using different data structure. I encourage you to read my friend's solution and determine which is best for you.

---

[29]http://www.emanueleferonato.com/2017/09/09/123-html5-game-made-with-phaser-updated-and-commented/

Game #1 code review

Reference	Play Game internal functions
1	Init function – not used
2	preload function – Lines 138 to 162
3	create function – Lines 163 to 233
4	update function – Lines 234 to 281
5	answeredQ function – Lines 282 to 299
6	btnOver function – Lines 300 to 327
7	checkAnswer function – Lines 330 to 351
8	gameOver function – Lines 352 to 362
9	nextQuestion function – Lines 363 to 395

NOTE: You can download this 8-page file from

http://makingbrowsergames.com/starterkits/quiz/v2_quiz_game1JS.pdf

Review this file; it is thoroughly annotated and documented to reduce the price of this pamphlet.

Exercise Game 1:

Take this exercise online[30]

Game #1 Creation — follow the instructions:

- Open the pdf file above in a new browser tab.

- Review the pdf content as you read the design considerations below.

- Now open your favorite source code editor and construct this play.js file.

- Build each of the listed functions.

- Lines 1 – 40: Administration, License and credit assignments.

---
[30]http://leanpub.com/courses/leanpub/mbg-dating/quizzes/game1

- Lines 41 to 62: global variables created for the game. I create a 5-answer button array as a lower HUD and float on top of each button a dynamic text label called 'AnswerTxt'.

- Lines 41 & 42: I keep the answer buttons separate from their labels.

- Line 44: I use the Golden Ration in all my games.

- Line 47: holds a variable to manage the internal game phases inside this single-state game. Yes, I lied. The game is really NOT a single state game.

- Line 49: sets the number of questions in the pool.

- Line 52: creates the dynamic question pool (database) for this game's session.

- Lines 55 & 56: I keep the question text displayed separately from its composition.

- Lines 59 to 62: one place to find all the text styles I use.

- Lines 64 to 95: Creates the question data structure pool and stores each question displayed. I randomly create the first and second numbers to "+". Read my design notes inside the source code for future enhancements. Generate the "correct answer (ca)" and assign a variety of "incorrect (wrong)" answers closely around the correct answer. I further randomize the answer pool per question so that the answer buttons won't always display the correct answer in the "3rd button".

- Line 93: save all the possible answers in an array from a "Fisher-Yates" shuffle.

  - Lines 91 to 94: provides a view into the question pool (database)

  - Lines 96 to 99: debug output

- Lines 100 to 124: is the "Fisher-Yates" shuffle routine.
- Lines 125 to 133: are the admin for the "game proper". It is divided into internal methods that control various phases of gameplay. The game presents the current question and waits for a response. The gamer will select their choice displayed on one of five answer buttons. When they click their choice, and an event will trigger a series of actions. This simple routine continues until the gamer arrives at the "maximum questions" configured for this question session.
- Lines 134 to 404: is the "so-called" single-state game object called "playGame".

preload function – Lines 138 to 162

- Lines 142 to 152 assume the same tasks as the normal 'boot.js'.
- Lines 153 to 162 are typical behavior for a 'preload.js' module

create function – Lines 163 to 233

The role of the creation phase is to prepare the various game assets for visual display from the cache. I add another responsibility at line 172; to search and find any previous games played and retrieve its high-score. Read through the source code comments for additional rationale.

- Line 176 to 181: create and deploy 5 answer buttons

- Lines 182 to 201: **the secret sauce!** Take 5 newly created answer buttons and build individual characteristic for each. Assign a unique name per button, create new value on this current question, scale and fix to the game board, and activate mouse listeners. Create a text label on top of each button and center this label.

- Lines 203 & 204: are for debugging and monitoring of these components.

- Lines 206 to 215: create and assign the first question from the question pool into the text components and assign text style attributes.

- Lines 216 to 219: create and assign the heads-up display.

- Lines 221 to 233: create and assign credits and copyrights.

update function – Lines 234 to 281

The update function manages the internal game phases through a simple switch statement. Provided that we have not reached the end of the questions in the pool, the game will refresh the text displays in the HUD, all the questions and their associated labels on the answer buttons. If we have reached the last (or beyond) question, we will simply display a "game over" notice.

- Line 247: Notice that I refer to the questions array length. If you decide to change the quantity of questions in a game session in the 'maxSum' variable, then the question array will dynamically re-adjust to that new variable. I simply hate using "hard-coding", and this illustrates how powerful "reference coding" truly is.

- Line 249: Notice the reference between "progress" and the internal question's index ('ndx'). I had a problem with the game skipping or counting by twos. This is a solution I used to ensure the proper question number was displayed. The problem I found was that Phaser is too fast (60 fps) and humans are too slow. There are other more elegant ways to do this.

- Lines 228 to 233: **Yes, I hardcoded this**. If you want more or less answers available, then you might adjust this to a better reference style. Currently as seen, its purpose is to update the labels floating on top of the answer buttons beneath during the update function. I chose not to destroy and recreate the all the text answers to every new question. Instead, I chose to simply change the text answers within the provided text labels.

4. Game #1 Supporting Functions

Lines 282 to the end are all the game supporting methods.

Use the "Developer's Console" to watch the internal operations of this game.

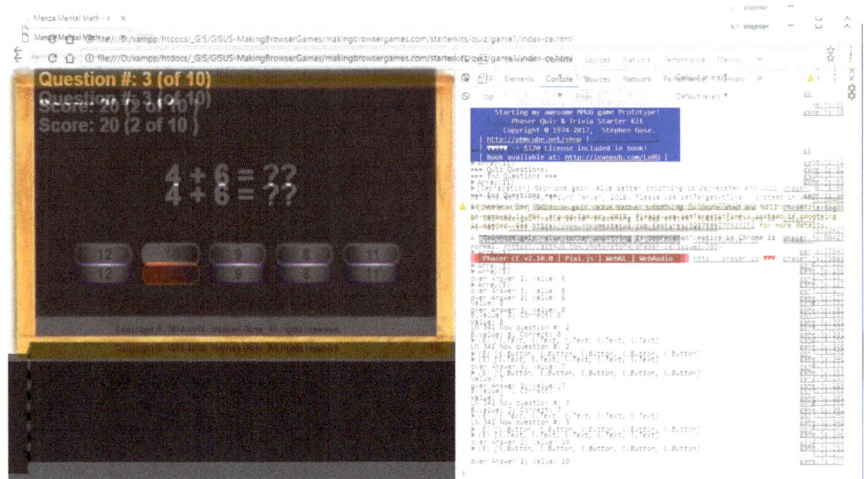

Game and Developer Console

NOTE: You can download this 8-page file from

http://makingbrowsergames.com/starterkits/quiz/v2_quiz_game1JS.pdf

Review this file; it is thoroughly annotated and documented to reduce the price of this pamphlet.

 These trivia games (in this tutorial) use only *Pure Vanilla JavaScript and Phaser Gaming Framework*.

Exercise Game 1 Supporting Functions:

Take this exercise online[1]

---
[1]http://leanpub.com/courses/leanpub/mbg-dating/quizzes/game1sf

Game #1 Supporting Functions

Game #1 Creation – follow the instructions:

- Open the pdf file above in a new browser tab.
- Review the pdf content as you read the design considerations below.
- Now open your favorite source code editor and append these supporting function to your play.js file.
- Build each of the listed functions.

answeredQ function – Lines 282 to 299

Lines 282 to 299: Because Phaser is so very quick – running a game at 60 fps – it might appear that the game is "stuttering" on an input button; when in reality, the human reactions are just too slow. The primary purpose of the 'answeredQ' function is to compensate for the speeds between humans and Phaser. Try an experiment and see what happens if this function is NOT referenced.

btnOver function – Lines 300 to 327

This is considered a 'debug' function to record which button the gamer is currently 'over' and the value assigned to this answer button.

checkAnswer function – Lines 330 to 351

The single purpose of this function is to validate the gamer's answer submitted to the calculated and correct answer stored inside this question object. Many lines are for debugging. Line 339 assigns a new internal game phase. If the two answers match; then award points to the score and increment the "correct answers". Finally, call the 'nextQuestion' function whether or not the gamer answered correctly.

gameOver function – Lines 352 to 362

This function manages the game's shut-down. It prepares a notice to the gamer, and stores the score into the local storage.

nextQuestion function – Lines 363 to 395

This is a "behind the scenes" worker. It increases our question "pointer" to the next question in the pool for display. It sets our game phase back to "displaying a question", and most importantly it updates the answer buttons' values and their associated labels with the new information. Salted inside are all console's debug displays to monitor proper actions. It further monitors when the gamer has reached the last question and assigns the appropriate internal game phase.

IV Game #2 – Tomfoolery Trivia Topics™ – a simple trivia game

Tomfoolery Trivia Topics™ is a Trade and service mark of Stephen Gose LLC. All rights reserved.

Trivia games have become so popular because they are easy to play, addictive and extremely easy to create in HTML alone. They also hold an "educational value", even if all you learn are a few trivial facts. Our trick is to bring a naturally text-based HTML game into the Phaser canvas as a rendered graphics. So, let us begin our simple trivia quiz by creating the game board, entities, and pieces for this heavily text-based game. This game will present a series of simple trivia questions as found in popular TV Game shows and pose possible answers – **all of this, from a remotely pre-generated question pool inside the gamer's browser!** Since text-based games are dependent on the gamer's native language, we'll present our standard language-selection menu first, then download all text for that chosen language. Furthermore, this game should follow the "traditional" format we discussed earlier in this chapter; it should be a "multi-state" game with responsive "mobile design". We will borrow ideas from game #1 as far as the questions' data structure, and internal sub-state processing. The following functions support the **Quiz & Trivia** game logic and manage user interactions. I have inserted them into the `play.js` since they are only required during the gameplay phase. I have used simple structural programming, but have grouped functions that could have become classes.

Please refer to your `main.js` as we dissect this game construction. You may download this bonus content from this book's website:

http://makingbrowsergames.com/starterkits/quiz/v2_quiz_game2_mainJS.pdf

Advertisement for Jester Costumes from

https://www.envycorner.com/mischievous-jester-costume-16219.html

Design Note:

Conveniently, this game follows the same design patterns as game #1. This maintains our "D.R.Y." approach. The only difference, between these two game editions, is that this game loads a remote question pool into either XML or JSON. XML is a little bit verbose, but we could fix that by shortening down the tags. The method for reading XML is similar to JSON, and I will focus on just JSON in this game's example.

Google recently (? 4 Oct 2016) announced that **Google Assistant** will open for developers and provide "Google Actions". I encourage you to research the mobile apps you can build using Google Actions. One such app is a "**Trivia App**" and template; you can read about it here[2]. It provides many coveted features such as question database editor, various audio personality voices, and many others "juicy" features that might spark your imagination as we build this Phaser trivia game.

We will use the data structure for individual questions from game #1. The primary aspects of a trivia game are: 1) the display of the individual questions; 2) the input answer menu; and 3) the HUD. All of these, we have created already in game #1. No doubt, there are thousands of ways to do this, but for this demonstration, I will use a simple text display for both questions and 4 possible answers labeled "1" to "4". I chose numbered answers because I cannot predict to whom and what language the game will present.

Database Construction Tools

For XML, I recommend Microsoft XML Notepad. It is open source and easy to use. XML Notepad 2007 is the latest release. Another option is the XAML tool integrated into Visual Studio. You can find it by searching for "xmlnotepad" or visit https://www.microsoft.com/en-us/download/details.aspx?id=7973

Download the following XML or JSON databases for game #2:

- XML: http://makingbrowsergames.com/starterkits/quiz/game2/assets/questions/ttt.xml
- Optional XML with hints & facts: http://makingbrowsergames.com/starterkits/quiz/trivia1.xml
- JSON: http://makingbrowsergames.com/starterkits/quiz/game2/assets/questions/jsonL0.json

Once you have this spiffy XML database file, you might like to convert it to JSON. I use this online tool[3] or you might like to pick your own.

---

[2] https://developers.google.com/actions/templates/trivia
[3] http://convertjson.com/xml-to-json.htm

Remote Question Pool Using AppML

A simple local question pool would have been sufficient for this game and similar to what we did in game #1. Google Actions uses an "Excel spreadsheet-style" for its question pool with similar data content which I plan to use, but we will create a JSON file for our question pool. *The data format will be like that used in game #1.* Also, I have decided to use the W3School's version of AppML[4] for this game's *remote question pool on my server.* AppML is far more technology than what this simple game demonstration demands, but it will provide a way to add more features if I choose to grow and upgrade this game edition into a deluxe version at some later time. Instead of AppML, we have another alternative in AngularJS. But let's first review AppML.

AppML stands for "Application Modeling Language". AppML runs in any standard HTML page; we will have to do some "tweaking" to display question inside the Phaser canvas. AppML was based on HTTP request communication between a web client and the web server. *The AppML-based system was launched in 2001, several months before schedule, as the world's first commercial AJAX application.* Thank goodness AppML provides full HTML, CSS, and JavaScript freedom. AppML makes it easy to create Single Page Applications (SPA) in a very clean and efficient way. We could revisit game #1 and easily adapt it to use AppML and retrieve generated math questions from a remote server. Originally AppML was abandoned by its creators in September 2007, but revived by W3Schools in 2015. Other potential data formats are listed below, and are compared at https://www.w3schools.com/js/js_json_xml.asp:

- XML — Extensible Markup Language is a markup language that defines a set of rules for encoding documents in a format that is both human-readable and machine-readable. This was a popular protocol at the turn of the millennium but has been replaced by JSON. It is very flexible text format derived from SGML (ISO 8879). Originally designed to meet the challenges of large-scale electronic publishing, XML is also playing an increasingly important role in the exchange of a wide variety of data on the Web and elsewhere. Learn more about XML at https://www.w3schools.com/xml/

- JSON — **JavaScript Object Notation** is an open-standard file format that uses human-readable

---

[4] https://www.w3schools.com/appml/default.asp

text to transmit data objects consisting of attribute-value pairs and array data types (or any other serializable value). It is a very common data format used for the asynchronous browser-server communication, including as a replacement for XML in some AJAX-style systems. JSON is a language-independent data format. It was derived from JavaScript, but as of 2017, many programming languages include code to generate and parse JSON-format data. The official Internet media type for JSON is application/json. JSON filenames use the extension .json. Learn more about https://www.w3schools.com/js/js_json_intro.asp

AppML is a modern JavaScript library for bringing data into HTML applications from W3Schools; it is free to use. No license is necessary. No installation is required. Even if you have never worked with web development before, you will find AppML very easy to use. If you are an experienced web developer, you will soon discover the power of AppML. The AppML language and syntax conform to XML nicely.

- AppML uses XML to describe Internet applications.
- AppML applications are self-descriptive.
- AppML is a declarative language.
- AppML is independent of operating systems.
- AppML uses AJAX asynchronous technology.
- AppML is Open Source.
- AppML is a language created and maintained by the W3Schools.

Building an AppML application

AppML applications are a simple to build. The AppML tutorial[5] could be summarized into this 4-step process.

1. Describe the elements of the application with AppML (style / XML conformance)
2. Save the XML file to a web server.
3. Link the file to an AppML Web service.

---
[5] https://www.w3schools.com/appml/default.asp

4. To change the application later, just change the contents of the XML file and save it, the web service will do the rest.

Skeleton XML format for Trivia Game Questions

```
1  <AppML>
2    <database>
3      <SingleQuestionItem>
4      <Question></Question>
5      <CorrectAnswer></CorrectAnswer>
6      <WrongAnswers></WrongAnswers>
7      <WrongAnswers></WrongAnswers>
8      <WrongAnswers></WrongAnswers>
9      <WrongAnswers></WrongAnswers>
10     <hints>not used</hints>
11     <facts>not used</facts>
12     <Aspects used in game #3 "Dating Veronica Darlene"™>
13       = are follow-on ideas of the same question (what next?)
14       = whether right or incorrect answer given (what next?)
15       = assuming different points of view (personalities?)
16       = assuming different points of view (asking or answering)
17       = assuming different background/circumstances/places
18     </Aspects>
19     </SingleQuestionItem>
20
21       : : : and so on . . .
22
23   </database>
24 </AppML>
```

Download the following XML databases for game #2:

http://makingbrowsergames.com/starterkits/quiz/game2/assets/questions/ttt.xml

Remote Question Pool Using JSON

Since AppML is basically the template engine part of AngularJS. Let's also consider using AngularJS and deliver JSON question pools. Research the following instructions:

https://phaser.io/news/2014/11/building-multiplayer-games-with-angular

Skeleton JSON format for Trivia Game Questions

```
1   {   "tttdb": {
2           "_Legal": "Copyright \u00A9 1978-2018, Stephen Gose. All Rights Reserved.",
3           "_GameVersion": "0.0.0.18",
4           "_GameTitle": "Tomfoolery Trivia Topics™ - a simple trivia game.",
5           "question": [
6               {
7                   "qText": "What is the fastest animal on Earth?",
8                   "ca": "Cheetah",                  //correct answer
9                   "ia": [                           //incorrect answer array
10                      "Spotted Leopard",
11                      "Giant Turtle",
12                      "Llama"
13                  ],
14                  "_category": "general",
15                  "_xtra": "1"
16              },
17          ], // . . . and so on . . .
18      }
19  }
```

Download the following JSON databases for game #2:

http://makingbrowsergames.com/starterkits/quiz/game2/assets/questions/jsonL0.json

Creating Various Languages

I am only able to translate games into a couple of languages based on my life experiences. I rely on Google Translate to assist with languages outside my education. I use a double check method when I use Google Translate. I start with my English text and have Google translate into my desired target language. I then reverse the process by taking their translation into a third language (French or Russian) and from the third language back into English. If the final English is satisfactory, I use the translation for my targeted language. Yes. It is time-consuming, but it worth the effort instead of mastering yet another language.

Game #2 code review

Reference	Play Game internal functions
1	Administrative – Lines 0 to 40
2	Play Scene variables – Lines 41 to 88
3	Init function – Lines 90 to 115
4	preload function – Lines 116 to 120
5	create function – Lines 121 to 193
6	update function – Lines 194 to 241
7	answeredQ function – Lines 242 to 259
8	btnOver function – Lines 260 to 287
9	checkAnswer function – Lines 288 to 311
10	gameOver function – Lines 312 to 318
11	nextQuestion function – Lines 319 to 352

NOTE: You can download this 7-page file from

http://makingbrowsergames.com/starterkits/quiz/v2_quiz_game2_playJS.pdf

Review this file; it is thoroughly annotated and documented to reduce the price of this pamphlet.

Exercise Game 2:

Take this exercise online[6]

Game #2 Creation — follow the instructions:

- Open the `pdf` file above in a new browser tab.

- Review the `pdf` content as you read the design considerations below.

- Now open your favorite source code editor and construct this `play.js` file.

- Build each of the listed functions.

---

[6]http://leanpub.com/courses/leanpub/mbg-dating/quizzes/game2

- Lines 1 – 40: Administration, License and credit assignments.

- Lines 41 – 88: global variables created for the game. I create a 5-answer button array as a lower HUD and float on top of each button a dynamic text label called 'AnswerTxt'.

   - Lines 42 & 43: I keep the answer buttons separate from their labels.

   - Lines 45 – 55: I offer a development choice in construction. I followed the in-memory model mentioned. There are advantages to using the other path. I'll let you explore and determine that best path for your game.

   - Line 53: The question array is built here in the playScene.

   - Lines 54 – 88 initialize the local variables and the same Fisher-Yates shuffling function.

Init function – Lines 90 to 115

This function is different than game #1. Here we prepare and load the JSON cached file into memory data structure. Game #2 is different in that we are loading text questions; whereas game #1 simply generated random mathematical equations. The questions are loaded into a question array similar as before, but having a different structure. I still shuffle the answers. The gamer will have a selection of 1 correct and 3 incorrect answers.

Notice how I use the JSON cached file. I load the cached information into the memory data structure with:

MovingJSONintoworkablememory

```
1   qText = this.game.cache.getJSON('jsonQFile').tttdb.question[i].qText;
2   //console.log(qText);        //debug
3   //correct answer
4   cA = this.game.cache.getJSON('jsonQFile').tttdb.question[i].ca;
5   //incorrect answers - hard coded
6   var iA1= this.game.cache.getJSON('jsonQFile').tttdb.question[i].iac[0];
7   var iA2= this.game.cache.getJSON('jsonQFile').tttdb.question[i].iac[1];
8   var iA3= this.game.cache.getJSON('jsonQFile').tttdb.question[i].iac[2];
9
10  // defining questions[i] as a composite of 3 array
11  // remember that arrays start counting from 0 not 1
12  //Design Note:
13  // this version is "locked" into 1 correct & 3 incorrect answers
```

```
14    questions[i]=;
15    //console.log(questions[i].allAnsw);        //debug
```

preload function - Lines 116 to 120

Nothing of interest here other than a console log.

create function - Lines 121 to 193

The role of the creation phase is to prepare the various game assets for visual display from the cache. I add another responsibility at line 129; to search and find other jester costumes for my client; this is disabled in our demonstration. Read through the source code comments for additional rationale.

- Lines 132 – 140: I create the input answer buttons for the gamer's responses. These are arranged vertically in contrast to game #1's horizontal arrangement.
- Lines 141 – 158: are similar to game #1. I am assigning properties to each answer button and an associated text label.
- Lines 165 – 173: set up the text-question from the in-memory data structure. Yes, I could have simply just "read" the raw JSON file at this point.
- Lines 174 – 177: set up the heads-up display with progress and scoring.
- Lines 178 – 190: sets up the copyrights notice in the code for display.

update function - Lines 194 to 241

As in game #1, the update function is the game engine. It serves the same process of updating all the text questions, buttons, labels and answers. It further adjusts to the current internal game sub-state.

Unlike game #1, this game engine correctly progresses to the "Game Over" phase.

5. Game #2 Supporting Functions

Lines 240 to the end are all the game supporting methods. Use the "Developer's Console" to watch the internal operations of this game.

Game Over Scene

NOTE: You can download this 7-page file from

http://makingbrowsergames.com/starterkits/quiz/v2_quiz_game2_playJS.pdf

Review this file; it is thoroughly annotated and documented to reduce the price of this pamphlet.

 These trivia games (in this tutorial) use only *Pure Vanilla JavaScript and Phaser Gaming Framework*.

Exercise Game 2 Supporting Functions:

Take this exercise online[1]

Game #2 Creation — follow the instructions:

- Open the `pdf` file above in a new browser tab.

- Review the `pdf` content as you read the design considerations below.

- Now open your favorite source code editor and append these supporting function to your `play.js` file.

- Build each of the listed functions.

answeredQ function – Lines 242 to 259

- Lines 242 to 259: Because Phaser is so very quick – running a game at 60 fps – it might appear that the game is "stuttering" on an input button; when in reality, the human reactions are just too slow. The primary purpose of the `answeredQ` function is to compensate for the speeds between humans and Phaser. Try an experiment and see what happens if this function is NOT referenced.

btnOver function – Lines 260 to 287

This is considered a `debug` function to record which button the gamer is currently `over` and the value assigned to this answer button.

checkAnswer function – Lines 288 to 311

The single purpose of this function is to validate the gamer's answer submitted to the calculated and correct answer stored inside this question object. Many lines are for debugging. Line 298 assigns a

---
[1] http://leanpub.com/courses/leanpub/mbg-dating/quizzes/game2sf

new internal game phase. If the two answers match, then award points to the score and increment the "correct answers". Finally, call the `nextQuestion` function whether or not the gamer answered correctly.

gameOver function – Lines 312 to 318

This function does nothing more than send the gamer to the next game phase. On the "Game Over" Scene, the gamer should find a button to return to the "mainMenu". This would be an excellent place to let the gamer submit their score, tweet of their accomplishments, review other's top scores or do online purchases.

nextQuestion function – Lines 319 to 352

This is a "behind the scenes" worker. It increases our question "pointer" to the next question in the pool for display. It sets our game phase back to "displaying a question", and most importantly it updates the answer buttons' values and their associated labels with the new information. Salted inside are all the console's debug displays to monitor proper actions. It further monitors when the gamer has reached the last question and assigns the appropriate internal game phase.

Use the "Developer's Console" to watch the internal operations of this game.

V Game #3 = Dating Veronica Darlene™

Dating Veronica Darlene™ is a Trade and service mark of Stephen Gose LLC. All rights reserved. in the studio, we affectional refer to this game as dating V.D. ;)

Mary-Ann Russon wrote this revealing article about "Otome Romantic Dating Simulator Games"[24] with over 22+ million gamers in 46 countries play these games. She provides targeting information and business deployment advice from leading developers who have cornered this game-style.

Now that we have created a few simple "text" trivia games with several game mechanisms such as generation, loading remote content, and validating answers, let's create a dating simulation = Dating Veronica Darlene!™[25] – originally derived from the former Winx Club Dating Sim. It will use various techniques we have learned from the previous two games.

This third version uses a lot of artwork, and since I am a horrible artist, I must rely on the talents of others. This game will present questions and answers from a larger question pool in multiple languages (text) along with the associated facial expressions (artwork).

So, let us begin our simple PG-rated dating game by creating the game board, entities, and pieces for this heavily text-based game

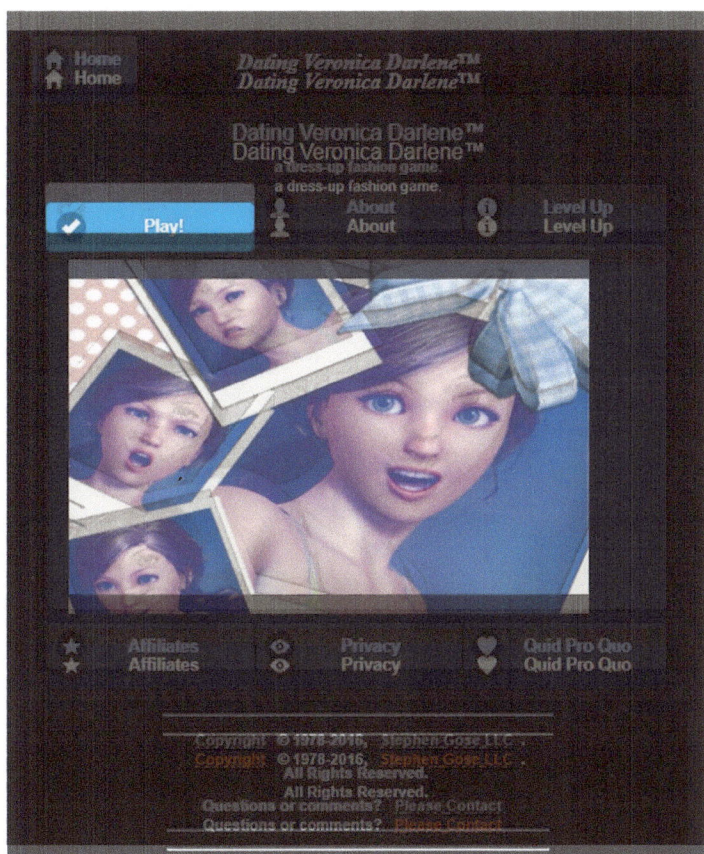

Dating Veronica Darlene™

Please refer to your main.js as we dissect this game construction. You may download this bonus 8-page content from the book's website:

http://makingbrowsergames.com/starterkits/quiz/v2_quiz_game3_mainJS.pdf

Design Notes:

This game[26] will present a series of questions typically occurring in a dating situation. Conveniently, this game also follows the same design patterns as found in our other game examples above = *all of this, from a remotely pre-generated question pool inside the gamer's browser! This follows our D.R.Y. Game Prototyping regimen.* The twist in this game is that the gamer will ask questions of the game's Artificial Intelligence represented by the Veronica personality. This should simulate a conversation dialog during a date's rendezvous. The gamer will select one of five "personalities" for Veronica in the active licensed game, and then select an initial place for their rendezvous. ***This demonstration game is locked to Veronica's "first" personality[27] and English language only.*** We can easily extend this simple game by adding more features from its original parent — Winx Club Dating Sims™ (2009-2012):

- Choice of gender to play — as a boy Specialist or girl Winx Club character, or create their own Winx character and save it into the member's "gallery". Members could then "date" each other.
- Whom to date — selecting the normal romance as seen in the popular cartoon series — or date another different character such as Trix, Winx, Specialist, or from the "members' gallery" of newly created characters by other game members. Perhaps allowing 2-player real-time interaction between online gamers of the same or different languages; this I never achieved, but it's still in the development milestones.
- Generate comic books from the rendezvous' encounter. Members could sale or give-away these comics.
- Generate a prologue and/or epilogue for an ongoing interactive story.

New conversation dialog format

The previous two trivia games were successful in consuming their XML and JSON question files. Let's not abandon that success. However, we must modify the question pool structure. We want this dating sims to take on a typical conversation dialog on a first, second and third date encounters. The gamer needs to **ask and answer questions**. We need a stage-play "script" similar to that of the Broadway theater or TV shows. The gamer will have "control" on ***what to ask and what to answer*** in the conversation dialog.

First Introduction Meeting

Conversation Dialog Sequence

A date will start with a "greetings", and then dive directly into Veronica (i.e.: the game's AI) asking questions, followed by the gamer asking questions of Veronica (i.e.: the game's AI). Each personality favors different responses as either "correct" or "inappropriate" answers. Players will score points from their answers and "appropriate questions asked". Veronica's facial expressions will provide immediate feedback whether points were earned or deducted. Incorrect answers are randomized (between 0 to -2) then applied to the Veronica *Facial Worksheet array.* Additional comments, "mood monitor", and Veronica's facial feedback will appear in the HUD (heads up display).

In the demonstration game, Veronica uses only one of her five (5) personalities, and English is the only available language. This English dialog file for "personality #1" is 24KB. In an "active licensed" game, Veronica personalities are randomized between 5 personalities or the gamer can select one of her five personalities for the current game session. There are separate language files for each of the five (5) personality. I chose to separate her personalities to facilitate the scoring and provide game asset security. I could have simply created one language file with all the various personalities within; but, filtering and scoring responses on the client-side would be quite a detailed process. Furthermore, a crafty person would be able to see how to win for any given personality in this monolithic file. And, a monolithic file would be 5x larger! This is a security consideration about *"how much of the game is available"* in the local browser cache at any time during a game session.

I use a 2D array as the "Broadway Theater" stage director. The rows in the array track the first, second and third date encounters. The columns track the conversation during that date encounter. Review the source code annotations for symbols and definitions.

Creating Various Languages

As I mentioned before, text-based games are heavily dependent on the gamer's native language; therefore, we'll present our standard language-selection menu first, then download all the text dialogue for that chosen language based on Veronica's chosen personality and rendezvous location. Furthermore, this game should follow the "traditional" format we discussed earlier in this chapter; it should be a "multi-state" game with responsive "mobile design". We will borrow the ideas from both games #1 and #2 as far as the questions' data structure – adding more features to support this unique gameplay and interactive dating dialog, and internal sub-state processing. We will add facial expressions as static images too.

 DAZ3D studio[2] also offers an "interactive license" for their facial expression tool-kits.

---

[2] https://www.daz3d.com/facial-expressions-for-v4

Language Selections are always displayed first

Game 3 updated question format

JSON was used successfully in game #2, we should adopt that solution and modify it to accommodate the new requirements in this game's logic. The gamer will have the opportunity to answer and ask questions. Veronica facial expressions will show her facial responses to answers and questions. So instead of merely having wrong answers as text, we will need to associate her facial responses too.

We will add a primitive artificial intelligence onto each of Veronica's personalities. Some personalities will favor certain attitudes, answers, and questions. Points will be rewarded or subtracted; the points will appear in the HUD as simple "hearts" or "broken hearts" icons with a "thermometer" between in the active licensed game. Our demonstration will use a simple "mood" thermometer.

The question format will include "aspects" – such as favorite or unfavorable dating locations that will influence the answers and questions final outcomes.

For correctly answered questions, Veronica will respond "joyfully". For wrong answers or simply bad questions asked of her, Veronica will respond with varying degrees of fear, anger, disgust, sadness, and surprise. Review the Veronica Work Sheet; it represents a two-dimensional array that I will use to pull Veronica's emotional responses. We could pull the images randomly or create an articulate formula; either way, the results should be entertaining.

I will add an aspect to scoring wrong answers. I will randomly generate a wrong answer score of 0, -1 or -2. I can use this to discover emotional reactions that are rated from mild to extreme. The benefit we gain is the gamer will always have an unpredictable session and response to "bad answers/questions".

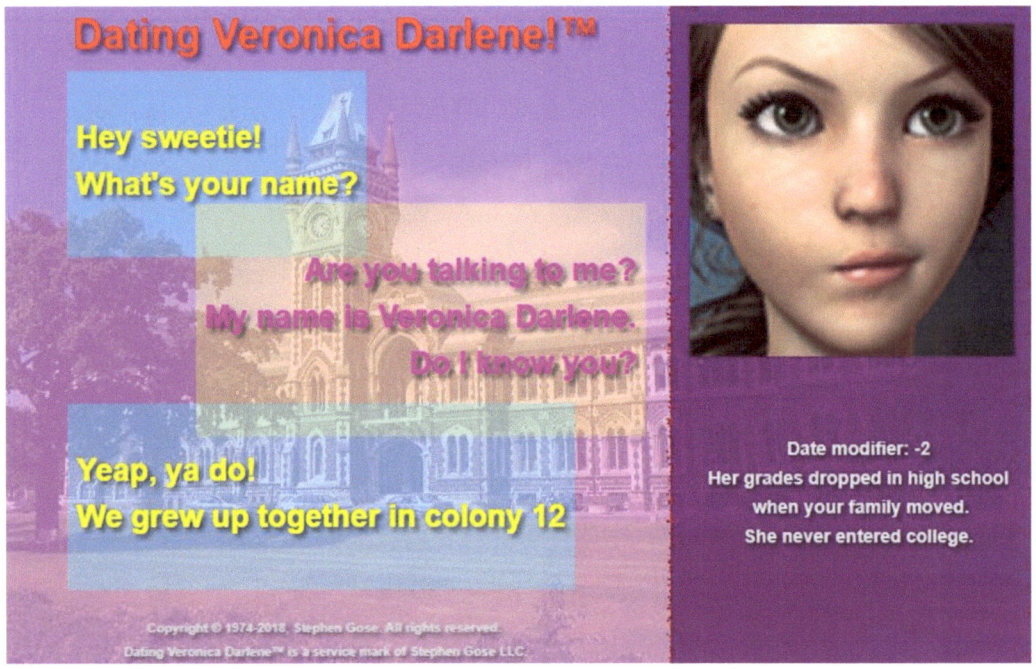

First Meeting in a bad place

Game 3 JSON format Skeleton

This is a high-level demonstration of the new question pool for this game. You can fill in new conversation content using this skeleton and use the same game logic. This is how I created all the various language files for each of Veronica's personalities.

Skeleton JSON format for Game #3 Scripted Dialogs

```
{
    "dvddb":{
        "_Legal": "Copyright © 1978-2018, Stephen Gose. All Rights Reserved.",
        "_GameVersion": "0.0.0.18 semvers",
        "_GameTitle": "Dating Veronica Darlene™ - a
                                    simple dating simulation game.",
        "_personality": "#1",
        "_lang": "English"

        //Veronica' favorite and non-favorite locations
        "place":[
            //array of 5 locations; index 0-2 are favorites
            // index 3-4 non-favorites; -1 and -2 respectively
        ],
        //date sequence
        "date": [
            //array for first, second, and third date greetings
            {
                "greetings":{
                    //first date
                    "default":[]
                    "rnd": []
                }
            },
            {
                "greetings":{
                    //second date
                    "default":[]
                    "rnd": []
                }
            },
            {
                "greetings":{
                    //third date
                    "default":[]
                    "rnd": []
                }
            }
        ],
        //date conclusion
        "invite":{
```

```
                        //ending of a date with random responses.
                        "default": [ ],
                        "rnd1":    [ ],
                        "rnd2":    [ ],
                        "rnd3":    [ ],
                        "rnd4":    [ ]
                },

                //Gamer's questions to ask Veronica; randomly selected between
                //   good and bad then removed (popped) from the pool.
                "askBad": [
                        //array of bad questions to ask Veronica
                        // these are randomly selected
                        //This is a modified format of games #1 and #2
                        {
                        "qText":   "What is your favorite color?",
                        "vdAnswer": "I'd have to say black, its so dark and emo."
                        },
                        // . . . etc. . . .
                ],
                "askGood": [
                        //array of good questions to ask Veronica
                        // these are randomly selected
                        //This is a modified format of games #1 and #2
                        {
                                "qText":   "Where do you usually shop?",
                                "vdAnswer": "I usually buy shirt-sand music at \
                                        the music venue from the bands I like."
                        },
                        // . . . etc. . . .
                ],

                //Veronica's questions to gamer
                "vdQues": [
                        //This is the same format as games #1 and #2
                        {
                        "qText":  "Have you seen that new tv show?",
                        "ca":     "It's so funny! I loved it when that guy got knocked out!",
                        "ia":     [
                        "Yes! I love it! I wonder if they will end up together.",
                        "TV shows are kinda boring you know...",
                        "No, I was busy with writing my new software program"
                        ],
```

```
86                    // . . . etc. . . .
87                };
88            ];
89        }
90  }
```

Download this JSON database skeleton for your own game #3 development:

http://makingbrowsergames.com/starterkits/quiz/game3/assets/questions/skeletonFileStructure.js

Game Pool Technology

I would like to control and upgrade this game's question pool's content. This is different from game #1 that dynamically generated question locally, and from game #2 that had a static question pool for each language. I could follow the same delivery as in game #2. But you may have noticed that game #2 does not support "offline" gameplay. To resolve that, I have decided to use an SQLite database on the gamer's side for several reasons in the licensed game. SQLite fits nicely in any mobile device and permits gamers to have the latest upgrades to the current question pool. Of course, this is far more technology than what this simple game demonstration demands but will provide a way to add more features as I grow and upgrade this game into its deluxe licensed version. Read about SQLite features and capabilities from their website here.[3] Other competing formats you might consider are:

- *Un-QLite*[4] — by the same author of SQLite, is an embeddable NoSQL database engine that I am toying with for future game development. SQL is 35+ years old; a recent trend in data storage is the migration to "document store" databases. A migration, I wish, WordPress would seriously consider.
- *PouchDB*[5] — my second choice and better suited to this game's size as it is currently demonstrated. PouchDB is an open-source JavaScript database inspired by Apache CouchDB that is designed to

---

[3] https://sqlite.org/about.html
[4] https://unqlite.org/
[5] https://pouchdb.com/

run well within the browser. It was created to help web developers build applications that work as well offline as they do online. It enables applications to store data locally *while offline,* then synchronize its content with CouchDB and compatible servers when the device and applications are back online, keeping the user's data in sync no matter where they next login. **Read more about this is my upcoming books on progressive web applications (PWA).**

- *TaffyDB*[6] — **was demonstrated in game #1** as we dynamically created a question pool of JavaScript objects. TaffyDB is an open source library bringing powerful database functionality to that concept and rapidly improve the way you work with data inside of JavaScript.

- *W3Schools AppML*[7] — **was demonstrated in game #2** as we created a question pool of JavaScript objects on our remote server.

Art Resources

This will be a short "PG Rated" game similar to that of *"Games2Win.com Speed Dating 2"*[8] but, instead of using cartoon characters, our artwork will come from *Daz3D*[9] using their *Aiko 5 model*[10] and a facial expression toolkit[28] for a more "life-like" interactions. These are old tools from my workshop and you may be interested in more updated and quite impressive technology illustrated below. The DAZ3D Genesis framework and facial expressions were designed to work on *any Daz3D Genesis model (life-like male or female, cartoon, anime or ethnic preference).* It has over 440 different facial expressions to use. The *Daz3D Studio is free*. Daz3D also has a variety of 3D people, places, environments and facial expression kits.[11]

---

[6] http://taffydb.com/
[7] https://www.w3schools.com/appml/default.asp
[8] http://www.games2win.com/en/romance-games/speed-dating-2-game.asp
[9] https://www.daz3d.com/home
[10] https://www.daz3d.com/aiko-5-premier-add-on-bundle
[11] https://www.daz3d.com/sans-pokerface-expressions-for-girl-6

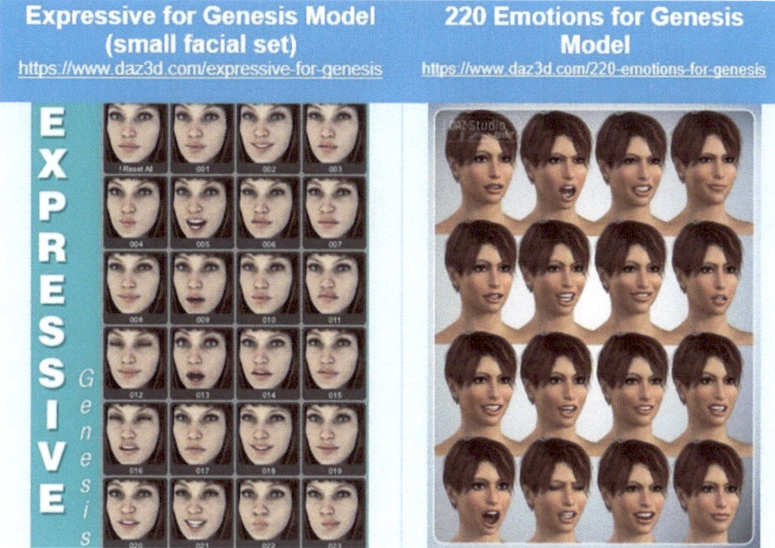

No Poker faces here!

Facial Expressions

This is a side-trip into facial expression and human emotions. How do we know which picture to use as good, favorable, poor, or inappropriate responses? Fortunately for us, Dr. Robert Plutchik has pioneered this research. Wikipedia states, "Robert Plutchik's psycho-evolutionary theory of emotion is one of the most influential classification approaches for general emotional responses. He considered there are eight primary emotions — anger,[12] fear,[13] sadness,[14] disgust,[15] surprise,[16] anticipation,[17] trust,[18] and joy.[19] Plutchik proposed that these 'basic' emotions are biologically primitive and have evolved to increase the reproductive fitness of the animal. Plutchik argues for the primacy of these emotions by showing each to be the trigger of behavior with high survival value, such as the way fear inspires the fight-or-flight response[20]." We can refer to his "wheel of emotions"

---

[12] https://en.wikipedia.org/wiki/Anger
[13] https://en.wikipedia.org/wiki/Fear
[14] https://en.wikipedia.org/wiki/Sadness
[15] https://en.wikipedia.org/wiki/Disgust
[16] https://en.wikipedia.org/wiki/Surprise_(emotion)
[17] https://en.wikipedia.org/wiki/Anticipation_(emotion)
[18] https://en.wikipedia.org/wiki/Trust_(social_sciences)
[19] https://en.wikipedia.org/wiki/Joy
[20] https://en.wikipedia.org/wiki/Fight-or-flight_response

in which he suggested that the 8 primary emotions are polarized. For example, joy versus sadness, anger versus fear and so on. Plutchik extended his theory as an explanation for psychological defense mechanisms.

We will use his research and that of many others in our dating simulation.

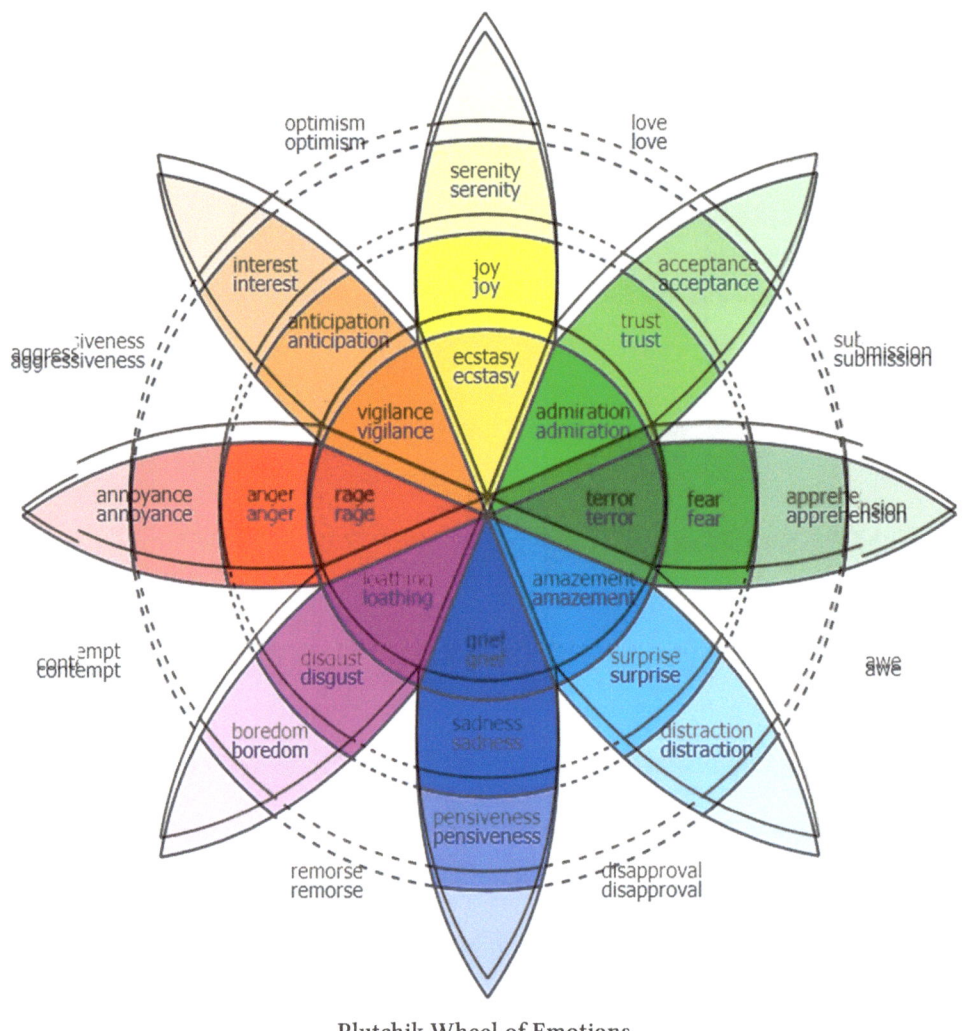

Plutchik Wheel of Emotions

So how are these emotions portrayed by human facial features? This article provides some ideas.[21] Yet, it doesn't provide a method to contrast and categorize all the facial expressions we need in our game. Wikipedia provides others who are researching face recognition and facial expressions. I

---

[21] https://www.interaction-design.org/literature/article/putting-some-emotion-into-your-design-plutchik-s-wheel-of-emotions

found these pictures from Wikipedia's supporting references.[22]

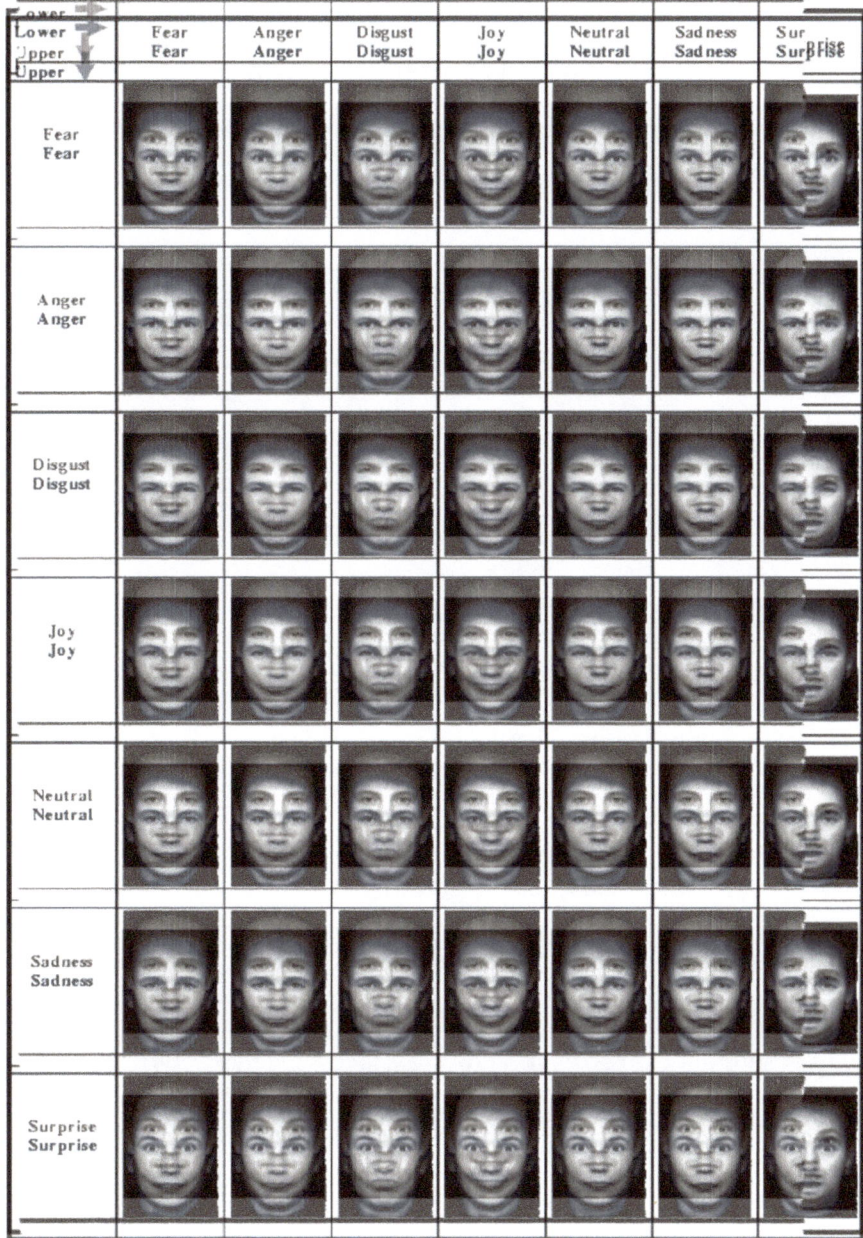

Computer Generated Prototypes of Facial Expressions of Emotion

https://www.dgps.de/fachgruppen/methoden/mpr-online/issue4/art3/node9.html

This chart shows a grid of 7x7 facial expressions cross-referenced to their underlying emotions. Analyze the combinations of "upper" facial features to their associated "lower" facial features by

---

[22] https://en.wikipedia.org/wiki/Contrasting_and_categorization_of_emotions

picking a column. Observe how the mouth (lower facial feature) is the same as you move up and down a column; however, the upper facial features (eyes and eyebrows) do change when moving up and down a single column. The combination of the upper and lower facial features reveals a single emotional reaction. Now select any row and move right and left. The upper face expression remains consistent, but the lower features changes.

Understanding this chart's construction provides the answers we need to match the correct facial expression to an image of emotional response to an answer from questions asked.

Emotion (E) = Facial Upper & Lower Mask (M) = Correct Response (C)

$$E = MC^2$$

Simple, right?

Download our Veronica Facial Expression worksheet here.

http://makingbrowsergames.com/starterkits/quiz/VeronicsWorkSheet.pdf

Our next task then becomes to compose all the game's questions, and then match Veronica's facial features to those text responses for each personality and language. At the beginning of each question, Veronica's facial expression will be in the "neutral upper" and "neutral lower" positions from the chart. After the gamer submits their answer, Veronica's face will change (with an "interactive license" we could tween?) into her emotional response.

Game #3 code review

Reference	Play Game internal functions
1	Administrative – Lines 0 to 40
2	Play Scene variables – Lines 41 to 89
3	Init function – Lines 100 to 254
4	preload function – Lines 255 to 282
5	create function – Lines 285 to 421
6	update function – Lines 422 to 468
7	answeredQ function – not used
8	btnOver function – not used; debug info only.
9	checkAnswer function – Lines 516 to 544
10	clickContinue function – Lines 546 to 671
11	gameOver function – Lines 674 to 678
12	nextQuestion function – Lines 681 to 713

NOTE: You can download this 14-page file from

http://makingbrowsergames.com/starterkits/quiz/v2_quiz_game3_playJS.pdf

Review this file; it is thoroughly annotated and documented to reduce the price of this pamphlet.

Exercise Game 3:

Take this exercise online[23]

Game #3 Creation — follow the instructions:

- Open the pdf file above in a new browser tab.

- Review the pdf content as you read the design considerations below.

- Now open your favorite source code editor and construct this play.js file.

- Build each of the listed functions.

- Lines 1 – 40: Administration, License and credit assignments.

---
[23]http://leanpub.com/courses/leanpub/mbg-dating/quizzes/game3

- **Lines 41 – 98:** global variables created for the game. I create a 5-answer button array as a lower HUD and float on top of each button a dynamic text label called 'AnswerTxt'.

- **Lines 43 & 65:** I keep the answer buttons separate from their labels. There's a lot going on in game #3. Veronica and the gamer have questions for each other. The gamer has both good and bad questions to present, and Veronica's reactions based on her current personality.

- **Line 52 – 55:** The question arrays are built here in the play Scene.

- **Lines 66 – 89** initialize the local variables and the same Fisher-Yates shuffling function.

Init function - Lines 100 to 254

This function is different than the previous games #1 and #2. I have preserved all the debug and console logging to help you to see the interactions. Here we prepare and load the JSON cached file into memory data structure. Game #2 is different in that we are loading text questions, whereas game #1 simply generated random mathematical equations. In game #3, we are loading a conversation dialog and game configurations. Uncomment the //**DEBUG sections and observe what happens in the console. The questions are loaded into the question arrays similar to before, but having a different structure. I still shuffle the answers. The gamer will have a selection of 1 correct and 3 incorrect answers. Veronica's responses are fixed responses for each conversation.

Notice how I use the JSON cached file. I load the cached information into the memory data structure with for loops. The loops parse through the entire collection and end when the array.length is completed. This is extremely flexible and permits me to add or delete conversations without tinkering with the source code.

preload function – Lines 255 to 282

Nothing of interest here other than a console log and selecting the specific date's location. Notice how I "overwrite" the background image with the current selection.

create function – Lines 285 to 421

Create gets rather involved and we should study what's happening.

- Lines 285 – 304: begin adding this date's location and Veronica's facial expressions modified by the dateModified – a general adjustment based on her favorite places. I added some filters to ensure her expression was within the 7x7 emotional chart.

- Line 302: selects the correct face from the spriteSheet.

- Lines 305 – 337: This process should familiar; it's the same process we used in game #2. It sets up the questions data structure for Veronica and moves everything off stage until needed after the greetings.

- Lines 338 – 419: Sets the various text boxes

update function – Lines 422 to 467

As in games #1 and #2, the update function is the game engine. It serves the same process of updating all the text questions, buttons, labels and answers. It further adjusts to the current internal game sub-state.

Unlike game #1, this game #3 game engine correctly progresses to the "Game Over" phase once all the dating sequence is concluded.

Notes

NOTES

24 Russon, M. (2014, May 21). 22 Million Women Worldwide Hooked on 'Otome' Romantic Dating Simulator Games. Retrieved August 04, 2017, from http://www.ibtimes.co.uk/22-million-women-hooked-otome-romantic-dating-simulator-games-1449353

25 This game is a derivative work of Stephen Gose Game Studio, from 2009 - 2011, Winx Club Dating Sim. Trade and service mark of Stephen Gose LLC. All rights reserved.

26 Affectionately nicknamed: "Dating V.D." inside our studio. This game is a derivative work from 2009, Winx Club Dating Sims.

27 I should have selected the girl's name as "Sybil" instead of "Veronica"; but, Archie comics were a strong influence in my childhood.

28 Technology never stops improving! Consider this updated version: https://www.daz3d.com/genesis-head-morph-resource-kit-1 or perhaps "sans-poker" face *my absolute favorite!*

6. Game #3 Supporting Functions

Lines 516 to the end are all the game supporting methods. Use the "Developer's Console" to watch the internal operations of this game.

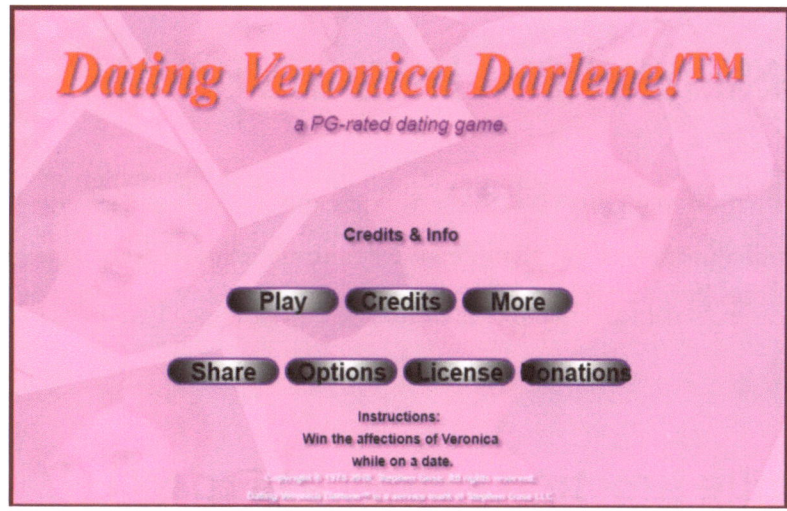

Dating VD Main Menu

NOTE: You can download this 14-page file from

http://makingbrowsergames.com/starterkits/quiz/v2_quiz_game3_playJS.pdf

Review this file; it is thoroughly annotated and documented to reduce the price of this pamphlet.

 These trivia games (in this tutorial) use only *Pure Vanilla JavaScript and Phaser Gaming Framework*.

Exercise Game 3 Supporting Functions:

Take this exercise online[1]

---
[1] http://leanpub.com/courses/leanpub/mbg-dating/quizzes/game3sf

Game #3 Supporting Functions

Game #3 Creation — follow the instructions:

- Open the pdf file above in a new browser tab.
- Review the pdf content as you read the design considerations below.
- Now open your favorite source code editor and append these supporting functions to your play.js file.
- Build each of the listed functions.

checkAnswer function - Lines 516 to 544

Minor adjusts to the new data structure names. Only questions from Veronica are "graded" and scored. Bad and rude questions from the gamer are automatically scored. Lines 528 to 540 include new code that modifies Veronica's facial expressions. Good or pleasing answers set the Lower facial mask with a smile.

clickContinue function - Lines 546 to 671

This is the "workhorse" of our game. I deployed it initially inside the update function but found it is not so taxing on the CPU here in its own function.
- Lines 547 - 550: handle the "game transitions, debug logging and game progress.
- Lines 561 - 661: are a series of if filters that catch the "Stage Director's script" cueing who's action it is and positioning text. Most of the work is stage directions moving components on and off the stage, positioning the correct dialog boxes and answer buttons.
- Line 668 - 669 moves to the nextQuestion function.

gameOver function - Lines 674 to 678

This function does nothing more than send the gamer to the next game phase. On the "Game Over" Scene, the gamer should find a button to return to the "mainMenu". This would be an excellent place

Game #3 Supporting Functions 81

to let the gamer submit their score, tweet of their accomplishments, review other's top scores or do online purchases.

nextQuestion function – Lines 681 to 713

This is a "behind the scenes" worker and performs similar tasks as found in game #2. It increases our question "pointer" to the next question in the pool for display. It sets our game phase back to "displaying a question", and most importantly it updates the answer buttons' values and their associated labels with the new information. Salted inside are all the console's debug displays to monitor proper actions. It further monitors when the gamer has reached the last question and assigns the appropriate internal game phase.

Use the "Developer's Console" to watch the internal operations of this game.

Plugins

Plugins are additional libraries that enhance your game. Many are found on Github.com by simply searching for "phaser".

 These trivia games (in this tutorial) use only *Pure Vanilla JavaScript and Phaser Gaming Framework*.

7. Conclusion

We are at the end of game development and should deploy our game into the wild. Topics such as launch times, download times, time to first byte (TTFB)[1], domain naming servers (DNS) lookups, all these now come into our business project's scope. When you launch a "Golden Release"[2], it is critical that we "collapse" all our module files into as few as possible, obfuscate them and minify them using Browserify[3]. I recommend several of these tools found in this workbook. "How to use such tools?", you say? Take a side-trip to this fantastic article. But you could also "copy-paste"; ensuring all the dependency are in the correct sequence.

More Game Starter Kit Tutorials

NOTE: This tutorial is a single chapter from a larger collection of game mechanics for both Phaser v2 and v3 found on http://leanpub.com/pgskc/ You can find all these Game Starter Kits for Phaser v2 and Game Starter Kits for Phaser v3 on Amazon.com. Search for Stephen Gose Phaser

Further Information

For those seeking more information about game design, ludology, gaming theory, mechanisms, and mechanics, there are references to these throughout this series of books. Information Technology is always a "moving target"; so I have provided a website with the most updated information, code corrections, and software updates.

http://makingbrowsergames.com/

---

[1] https://blog.cloudflare.com/ttfb-time-to-first-byte-considered-meaningles/
[2] http://www.webopedia.com/TERM/G/gold_version.html
[3] http://browserify.io

Introduction References

Let's conclude this chapter with related resource references available through LeanPub[4] and Amazon International[5].

- Supporting website and bonus content: http://makingbrowsergames.com/starterkits/

- Game Design Workbook (LeanPub)[6] or from Amazon Paperback[7] or Kindle / mobi / epub editon[8],

- Phaser Game Prototypes (LeanPub)[9] or coming soon to Amazon[10],

- Phaser Game Development Library (Bundled offer by LeanPub)[11],

- Ultimate Phaser Library (Bundled offer by LeanPub)[12]

- Individual Phaser Game Startkit chapters from Amazon for Kindle[13] or Amazon International Paperback[14].

---

[4]https://leanpub.com/u/pbmcube
[5]https://www.amazon.com/s/ref=nb_sb_noss_2?url=search-alias%3Daps&field-keywords=stephen+gose
[6]https://leanpub.com/phaserjsgamedesignworkbook
[7]http://amzn.to/2eXtUX4
[8]http://amzn.to/2xXk7oP
[9]https://leanpub.com/LoRD
[10]http://makingbrowsergames.com/book/
[11]https://leanpub.com/b/phasergamedevelopment
[12]https://leanpub.com/b/ultimatephaserlibrary
[13]http://amzn.to/2fci20g
[14]http://amzn.to/2gV5CtJ

VI Answers to Exercises

Making Dating \& Quiz Games

Lesson: Game Mechanics

1:

Lesson: Game Examples \& Research

1:
2:

Lesson: Game Flow

1:
2:
3:

Game \#1 = Menza Mental Math™: a math tutor game.

1:

Game \#1 Supporting Functions

1:

Game \#2 = Tomfoolery Trivia Topics™ = a simple trivia game

1:

Game \#2 Supporting Functions

1:

Game \#3 = Dating Veronica Darlene™

1:

Game \#3 Supporting Functions

1:

www.ingramcontent.com/pod-product-compliance
Lightning Source LLC
Chambersburg PA
CBHW051915210526
45473CB00006B/2018